Cancun and Mayan Riviera

The Ancient Mayan Ruins of Tulum

5-Day Itinerary

3rd Edition

By Ted Campbell

Table of Contents

Welcome to Cancun and the Mayan Riviera..................5
   How to Use This Guide..................7
Day 1..................11
   11:00 am -- Beach Day at Playa Delfines..................18
   12:30 pm -- El Rey Ruins..................20
   2:00 pm -- Mayan Museum and San Miguelito Ruins. 23
   3:30 pm -- More to Explore in the Zona Hotelera.......24
   5:00 pm -- Downtown Cancun..................28
   5:15 pm -- Mercado 28..................32
   6:30 pm -- Parque Las Palapas..................34
   8:00 pm -- Night Out in Cancun..................35
   Extra Time in Cancun..................35
Day 2..................37
   Overview -- Valladolid..................37
   10:30 am -- Get a Hotel in Valladolid..................40
   11:40 am -- Brunch at Bazar Municipal..................42
   12:40 pm -- San Roque Museum..................45
   2:00 pm -- Cenote Zací..................47
   3:10 pm -- Municipal Market..................49
   4:30 pm -- San Bernardino de Siena Convent..................53
   6:00 pm -- Valladolid by Night..................54
   7:00 pm -- Chichén Itzá Night Show..................56
Day 3..................60
   Overview -- Chichén Itzá..................60
   8:00 am -- The Mayan Ruins of Chichén Itzá..................62
   8:00 pm -- Quinta Avenida—Fifth Ave..................72
Day 4..................75
   8:00 am -- Playa del Carmen..................75
   12:20 pm -- Xaman-Ha Bird Sanctuary..................80
   2:00 pm -- Shopping on Quinta Av..................82
   4:00 pm -- Papantla Flyers and Other Entertainment. 84
   6:00 pm -- Dining in Playa..................86
   9:00 pm -- Night Out in Playa Del Carmen..................89

- Day 5 93
  - Overview -- Tulum 93
  - 9:30 am -- Dos Ojos Cenote 96
  - 12:20 pm -- The Mayan Ruins of Tulum 98
  - Goodbye Mexico 100
- Other Places to Go 101
  - Puerto Morelos 102
  - Cozumel, Isla Mujeres, and Holbox Islands ... 104
  - Beaches 110
  - Ruins 111
  - Adventure Ecoparks 114
  - Mérida 117
- Things You Need to Know 121
  - A Brief History 122
  - When to Go 124
  - Transportation 125
  - Hotels 136
  - Restaurants 139
  - Food and Drinks 141
  - Water 147
  - Money Matters 149
  - Haggling + Tipping 150
  - Safety 151
  - Useful Spanish Phrases 153
  - Places and Terminology 155
  - Links and Online Resources 157
- About the Author 164
- Unanchor wants your opinion! 167
- Other Unanchor Itineraries 168

Welcome to Cancun and the Mayan Riviera

You can smell the sea from the Cancun airport. No more stuffy airplane, no more boring job in your cold hometown. Welcome to paradise—the Mayan Riviera. Welcome to Cancun.

The Mayan Riviera is a 130-km (80-mile) stretch of Caribbean coastline in southeast Mexico. Between Cancun to the north and the Mayan ruins of Tulum to the south are countless white-sand beaches on the gorgeous turquoise water of the Caribbean.

Tourism began in the 1970s in the Mayan Riviera, especially in its unofficial capital Cancun. Cancun has since become famous for all-inclusive luxury resorts, while formerly lesser-known beach hangouts like Playa del Carmen are now firmly established on the beaten path.

But a budget-conscious side remains in these world-class tourist destinations. You can still get a nice hotel room for under $30 USD in downtown Cancun or just a few blocks from the beach in Playa del Carmen. And for the best, most authentic food—what the locals eat—you'll pay less than at McDonald's.

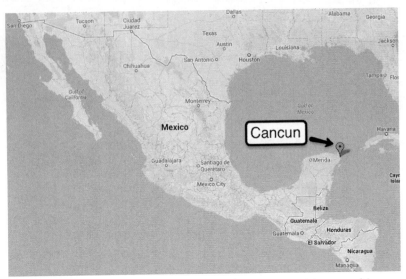

The Mayan Riviera is so interesting that you could even skip the beach and still have a great time. Visiting Mayan ruins is high on everyone's list. The Mayans were an advanced civilization that built great cities more than a thousand years ago. One of the greatest, Chichén Itzá, is now one of the new Seven Wonders of the World. Chichén Itzá and other ruins (like Tulum) are only a few hours from Cancun on good highways.

There aren't any mountains on the Yucatán Peninsula (where the Mayan Riviera is located at the easternmost part of Mexico), just lush, vivid-green jungle. This massive jungle grows out of porous limestone—so porous that a huge freshwater system of sinkholes, caves, and underground rivers is found throughout the peninsula. Called *cenotes*, many are open for swimming, snorkeling, and scuba diving.

Finally, culture is a big reason why Mexico is celebrated worldwide as a fantastic tourist destination. In the Mayan Riviera, you not only experience the rich Mexican culture, but local *yucateca* culture too. As a local may remind you, yes you are in Mexico, but you are in the Republic of the Yucatán as well.

How to Use This Guide

There's a lot to see in the Mayan Riviera, but if you only have a week, I recommend traveling in a triangle between Cancun, Chichén Itzá, and Playa del Carmen. They're surrounded by many other places to see, such as colonial towns, Mayan ruins, *cenotes*, islands, secluded beaches, and adventure parks.

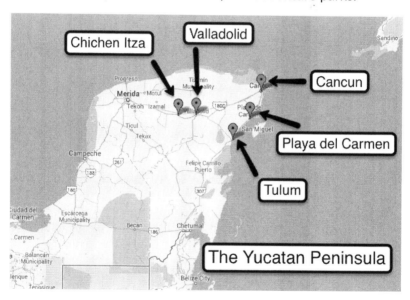

Spending the night in Valladolid before heading to Chichén Itzá will not only give you a jump on all the tour groups visiting the popular ruins, but you'll also get a taste of local culture and history in the lovely Spanish-colonial town.

Besides being a fun destination in its own right, Playa del Carmen is an excellent base for visiting the seaside ruins of Tulum, the island of Cozumel, and many different *cenotes*, along with options for day trips to ecoparks and lesser-known beaches. Descriptions, directions, and suggestions for these places can be found in the Appendix, along with information about hotels, transportation, food, culture, speaking Spanish, safety, managing your money, and much more.

In sum, this five-day itinerary takes you to the five major highlights of the region: Cancun, Valladolid, Chichén Itzá, Playa del Carmen, and Tulum, and it includes enough nearby alternatives to keep you busy for weeks.

If you have fewer than five days, you'll have to make decisions: for example, choosing only one ancient city. Tulum is smaller and closer than inland Chichén Itzá, which means that you can see it in only half a day. Or, if you skip Valladolid (and rent a car), you can get to Chichén Itzá and back (from either Cancun or Playa del Carmen) in a long day trip.

If you have more time, like a week or two, you can slow down and spend extra days in the places on this itinerary, especially Valladolid for culture or Playa del Carmen for restaurant and nightlife options. Or, you could spend a few nights at a low-key beach town like Puerto Morelos or Akumal.

It all depends on what you're interested in. Would you like to see more ruins, take a trip to an island, go shopping in an air-conditioned mall, have a spa day, check out museums, spend the day at a big adventure park, swim in less-visited *cenotes*, or take your kids to a water park, zoo, or nature reserve?

Would you like to scuba dive, snorkel, go fishing, go kite boarding, windsurf, golf, mountain bike, explore an underground river, or relax on a beach that's less developed than Cancun or Playa del Carmen? All of these are readily available, with prices ranging from free (a day at the beach) to inexpensive (small *cenote*parks, ferries to Cozumel and Isla Mujeres, most museums) to pricy but reasonable (spas, golf, fishing charters).

Whatever you decide, please don't feel like you have to do everything. In fact, you'll never do everything—there's way too much; you'd need six months, a year, or a lifetime. It's better to just choose a few things and enjoy them without feeling pressured, instead of hurrying around trying to squeeze it all in.

The order of this guide is what I consider the most logical sequence for visiting these five highlights of the Mayan Riviera. Feel free to change the order, do it backwards, skip a few things, and add others. Use the times between places as a reference, rather than forcing yourself to get going at 7 a.m. every day.

I give instructions for using public transportation, but you could easily rent a car to get around, which may be a good idea if you're traveling with kids or in a big group. Please see **Transportation** in the Appendix for information on car rentals.

On the walks, I've given ample time for slow walking, taking pictures, and ducking into a shop on the way. For the bus trips, I've followed the times given by the ADO bus company on its website. Please be flexible regarding these times, as you never know what could happen—the bus could leave late or there may be traffic, among other unexpected delays.

Day 1

============

Day 1 begins at 9 a.m. with a bus ride from the Cancun airport to downtown Cancun. Unless you actually do pick upyour luggage, get through customs, and get a bus ticket by 9 a.m., you obviously won't be able to use the exact timeline for **Day 1**.

If you arrive in the afternoon, for example, simply follow the instructions for getting into downtown and finding a hotel, and then take a look at the other activities described. Do you want to do them that evening or save them for the next day?

Cancun

There are two Cancuns, and when vacationers talk about Cancun, they usually mean the long thin island of powdery beach and big resorts overlooking the calm Caribbean. In Spanish, this part of Cancun is called the Zona Hotelera—the Hotel Zone.

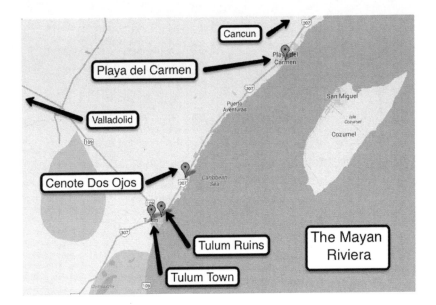

Downtown Cancun is on the mainland, a 20- to 30-minute bus ride from the Zona Hotelera and the beach. By staying downtown you can find better prices on everything, including hotels, restaurants, and souvenirs. Departing for Valladolid the next day will be easy because many budget hotels are near the downtown bus terminal.

If you want to stay in a resort in the Zona Hotelera, by all means do so. Please see **Hotels** in the Appendix.

9:00 am -- Bus from the Airport to Downtown Cancun

- **Price:** MXN $72.00 (for a single adult)
- **Duration:** 30 minutes

At the airport, walk past the booths for taxis, car rentals, and tours in the baggage claim area. Look for ADO—the name of the bus to take into downtown Cancun.

You can get a ticket at the booth inside or at another booth outside near the bus stop. Buses leave every half hour and the ride takes about 30 minutes. The bus may make a few stops, but don't get off until it pulls into the ADO bus terminal in downtown Cancun.

Note: *There are three terminals in the Cancun airport, each for different airlines. ADO buses leave from all three terminals so it's not so important to know which terminal you arrive at, but it's crucial when you depart so you get off the bus at the correct one. See* **Transportation** *in the Appendix for details about the Cancun airport.*

You can check the schedule at the ADO website. I don't recommend buying tickets in advance, however, in case your flight arrives late and you miss the bus. But if you do buy online, you can choose your seat and print the tickets beforehand.

If you arrive during high season (see **When to Go** in the Appendix), the line for bus tickets may be quite long. If it's really busy then tickets for the next bus may be sold out and you'll have to take the next one. If you don't want to wait, look at the prices of taxis, either posted in the booths or listed in a little folder. You can't miss the taxi booths—as soon as you look in their direction the attendants will start waving and calling out "taxi, taxi!"

The prices are determined by which area of the city you are going to. For downtown Cancun, look for the prices for *centro*. If you're going to a resort in the Zona Hotelera, tell them which one. Prices at different booths should be similar, but feel free to compare. Also, as they are per trip, not per person, you can try to find people to share with if you're all going to the same area.

If you have reservations at a resort in the Zona Hotelera and don't want to pay for a taxi all the way to your hotel, you can take the ADO bus to downtown Cancun and then take a local bus to your hotel. (Follow the directions to get to the beach.) This will take more time but will definitely be cheaper. On the second bus, from downtown Cancun, tell the driver the name of your hotel—most drivers are friendly and happy to help. Local buses from downtown Cancun to the hotel zone cost 10.5 pesos.

9:30 am -- Get a Hotel in Downtown Cancun

- **Duration:** 1 hour

In this itinerary, you stay in downtown Cancun. Many budget hotels can be found near the ADO bus terminal and from there catching a local bus to the Zona Hotelera (and the beach) is easy.

Compared to the big resorts on the beach, these hotels are pretty basic. But even the cheapest should have hot water, air conditioning, and a TV.

If you want to make reservations, check their websites for contact information or use booking.com or any travel booking site you like. But in the low season, you can arrive without reservations if you don't mind spending a little time walking around and looking at hotels. This has several benefits, as you can see the room before you take it and try asking for a discount.

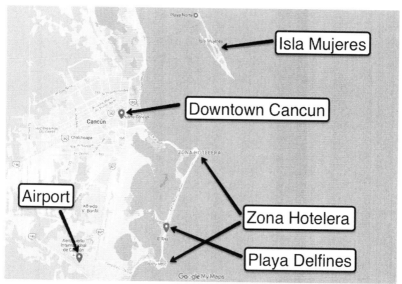

The ADO bus terminal in downtown Cancun is a good reference point. From there you can walk in any direction to find hotels and hostels. Below are my recommendations, and you'll pass many more on this walk. Please remember that prices are bound to change:

1. If you just want a cheap place to crash in a room full of bunk beds, the closest hostel to the bus station is Mundo Joven.
2. Las Palmas Hotel is cheap and clean, and it has a kitchen. It's 380 pesos for a single and 420 for a double in both high and low seasons.
3. Rooms at the Ramada are usually around 1,400 pesos. Sure, it's a little pricy, but it has a pool and all the amenities you'd expect from an international chain.
4. At a slightly lower price than the Ramada (1,150 pesos single/double in the low season), the Xbalamqué Hotel, Resort & Spa has more style and a local atmosphere.

5. On the southern end of Parque Las Palapas, Hotel Suites Cancún Center offers good value with big discounts, with a single or double for as low as 600 pesos per night. (Their official, posted prices may be higher, though.)
6. There are more hotels all around this area, including both cheap and mid-range ones on the way to Mercado 28. Another option from Parque las Palapas is to walk to Tulum Av and then keep wandering.

For this walk, leave the ADO bus terminal, walk across the parking lot, and go left on short Pino street. Then take a right on Uxmal Av, where you'll pass Mundo Joven and several other hotels. For Las Palmas, take a right on the second Palmera St, two blocks past Mundo Joven.

At Palmera St you'll see a busy intersection. Take a left there onto Yaxchilán Av and walk a few blocks, passing the Ramada and Xbalampué. Turn left immediately after Xbalampué to find Parque las Palapas, a nice place to take a break and eat in the food stands.

10:30 am -- Bus from Downtown to the Zona Hotelera

- **Price:** MXN $10.50 (for a single adult)
- **Duration:** 30 minutes

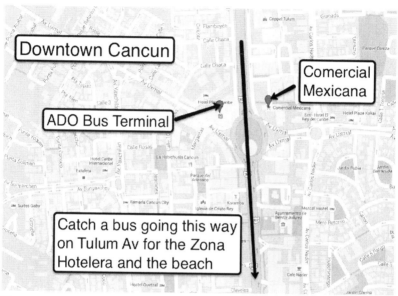

To get to the beach from downtown Cancun, catch any bus going south on Tulum Av with "Zona Hotelera" written on the windshield.

Keep an eye open for your destination through the big bus windows. But, to be sure you'll end up at the right place, you can ask the driver to stop there, for example at Playa Delfines:

- *¿Nos podemos bajar en playa delfines por favor?*
  Can we get off at Playa Delfines please?

Sit or stand near the driver so he doesn't forget about you. Most drivers are helpful and friendly, but if you get one who seems like he doesn't care, try asking one of the locals on the bus instead.

The ride to the Zona Hotelera takes 20 or 30 minutes, depending on how far down the island you go.

Tip: *Before you go to the beach, buy what you want for the day in downtown Cancun. Everything in the Zona Hotelera costs more: water, beer, food, sunblock, etc., and Playa Delfines is a little far from any stores. Look for Comercial Mexicana, a large, Walmart-type store across Tulum Av from the ADO bus terminal. To save money, buy something for lunch here because all the restaurants at the Zona Hotelera are pricy.*

11:00 am -- Beach Day at Playa Delfines

- **Price:** FREE
- **Duration:** 1 hour and 30 minutes
- **Address:** Km 19.5 Blvd Kukulkán, Zona Hotelera, Cancun

If you are like me, then after that long plane ride, you want to go straight to the beach. All of the Zona Hotelera is on the beach—long, wide, and overflowing with 22 km (14 miles) of powdery white sand. According to Mexican law you can go anywhere, regardless of which hotel lurks behind. But you need an access point to reach it. They pass between big hotels. Look for a blue sign with a beach on it that reads *Acceso a Playa*— beach access.

Playa Delfines (Dolphin Beach) is a locals' favorite near the southern end of the Zona Hotelera. Behind are big bluffs, and small shelters provide shade. You won't hear loud music from a resort pool. The swimming is fantastic.

There aren't any restaurants at Playa Delfines, though guys frequently walk down the beach with coolers full of food. For 10 pesos you can get some empanadas or tacos. If you want to go to a restaurant, look for them all along Boulevard Kukulkán, especially at big malls likeLa Isla or around Playa Caracol. Or, to save money, hold out for downtown Cancun.

You can stay at the beach all day, but if you get restless, there's a lot more to see in the Zona Hotelera, including Mayan ruins, museums, shopping malls, and marinas. You can take the local bus to these places (make sure you catch it on the correct side of the road), walk on Boulevard Kukulkán, or—my favorite—take the beach.

Tip: *If you plan on exploring the Zona Hotelera with multiple bus rides, bring a pocketful of coins to pay the bus fare. Ask for* cambio en monedas *(change in coins) the first time you buy water or beer at a convenience store.*

If you wave down a taxi, remember to negotiate the fare beforehand, as they don't have meters. If you don't speak Spanish, use a pencil and paper to write down numbers and expect a little overcharging. No ride in the hotel zone should cost more than 50 or 100 pesos.

Bring your own Frisbee to Playa Delfines:

12:30 pm -- El Rey Ruins

- **Price:** MXN $50.00 (for a single adult)
- **Duration:** 1 hour
- **Address:** Km 18 Blvd Kukulkán, Zona Hotelera, Cancun

You can catch your first glimpse of Mayan ruins at El Rey, a small but scenic site full of iguanas. It's across the road from Playa Delfines, with the entrance about 10 minutes south of the lookout at the northern end of the beach. Turn left on

Boulevard Kukulkán, walk past the Playa Delfines parking lot, and look for the clearly-marked entrance to El Rey at kilometer 18.

The ruins are open every day from 8 a.m to 5 p.m. with the last access at 4:30 p.m. The entrance fee is 50 pesos, and you can hire a guide for about 100 pesos.

Besides ancient stone structures and iguanas, the area also contains numerous native trees and plants, making for a lovely afternoon stroll. *El Rey* means "the king," the name coming from a stone sculpture that's now housed in the nearby Mayan Museum.

Don't forget to bring sunblock, insect repellent, and lots of water. And your camera, of course.

To check for updates on prices and schedules, see the page for El Rey on the website for the Mexican Secretary of Culture. It's in Spanish but times and prices should be obvious.

1:30 pm -- Walk to the Mayan Museum and San Miguelito Ruins

- **Duration:** 30 minutes

Walk about one mile north on Boulevard Kukulkán (to kilometer 16.5) to get to the Mayan Museum. It should take between 20 and 30 minutes, depending on the heat and your enthusiasm. You'll pass the big Iberostar Golf Club on the left.

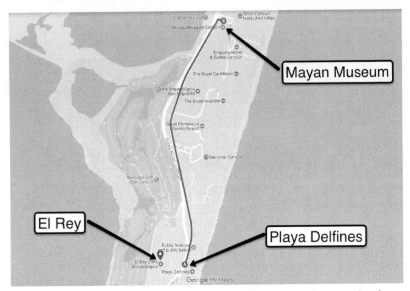

You'll see several bus stops, so hop on if you get hot or tired. Or if you'd like, you can try walking up the beach from Playa Delfines. To get to the museum, look for the sandy path between the Omni Hotel and Grand Oasis Resort, though the gate might be closed. This access point is a little farther north than the museum, so once you get to the road, take a left or ask anyone for directions to the *museo*.

If you get totally lost you can try cutting through a hotel lobby. In general, you'll have better luck doing this if you ask permission with a big smile, saying you want to go to the museum, instead of attempting to sneak through.

2:00 pm -- Mayan Museum and San Miguelito Ruins

- **Price:** MXN $70.00 (for a single adult)
- **Duration:** 1 hour and 30 minutes
- **Address:** Km 16.5 Blvd Kukulkán, Zona Hotelera, Cancun

For more on all things Mayan, visit the Cancun Mayan Museum (Museo Maya de Cancún), which opened in 2012. You can see lots of artifacts and get a history lesson in preparation for bigger ruins like Tulum and Chichén Itzá. The building has large windows with nice views of the green grounds, and it's air-conditioned too.

Admission costs 70 pesos and includes access to the San Miguelito ruins. It's open from 9 a.m. to 4:30 p.m. Tuesday-Sunday. Yes, **the museum is closed on Monday.**

The San Miguelito ruins, named after a ranch that was on the site from the 1950s to the 1970s, is a little south of the museum. Take the sandy, shady walking path through the jungle to get there.

To check for updates on prices and schedules, refer to the page for San Miguelito on the website for the Mexican Secretary of Culture.

Tip: On Sundays, Mexicans get in free to the Mayan Museum and many other museums and ruins, including Chichén Itzá. So, if you're Mexican, be sure to bring your IFE or other government ID, and if you're not, perhaps go on another day to avoid crowds.

3:30 pm -- More to Explore in the Zona Hotelera

- **Duration:** 1 hour

Shopping

On the way to Playa Delfines, once you are on the island proper, your first glimpse of the Zona Hotelera will be the area around Playa Caracol (Conch Beach, though *caracol* also means snail). You can't miss this cluster of pubs, beer-and-nacho spots, and nightclubs, including Coco Bongo, Señor Frogs, and the Hard Rock Café (the restaurant, not the resort).

You can visit the Plaza Caracol mall for some shopping, though if you want souvenirs, t-shirts, or Mexican handicrafts, Mercado 28 in downtown Cancun has a better selection and much better prices.

If you plan on going to huge nightclubs later, this is the area in the Zona Hotelera to check out. Take a look at the clubs and see if you can get discounted tickets.

Also in the Playa Caracol area, near the northeastern tip of the island, Delphinus Punta Cancun is a water park where you can swim with dolphins. Check their website for prices and other locations in the Mayan Riviera.

If you can't get enough shopping, for sure check out La Isla (the island), another shopping center south of Playa Caracol. It's all outdoors and built around canals, and it has a decent selection of restaurants.

At the entrance to La Isla is the Interactive Aquarium, which though small is a fun place to visit with kids, with dolphin shows and lots of colorful sea creatures. And roughly across the street, next to the Westin Hotel, is yet another Mayan site, Yamil Lu'um. Ask at the Westin visitor center for permission to check out the tiny ruin complex.

South of La Isla, concluding our mall tour is Kukulcan Plaza, a rather standard indoor shopping center with all the usual suspects: fashion, souvenirs, restaurants, and the Soriana supermarket for groceries, beer, and water.

At the southern end of Kukulcan Plaza is Luxury Avenue which, as the name suggests, is all about high-end stores like Louis Vuitton. See if they'll let you browse in your wet clothes and sandy flip-flops.

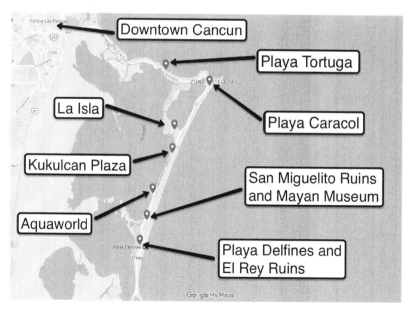

Ferry Terminals, Water Sports Complexes, and More

Right away as the road enters the thin strip of land leading to the island you'll pass the Cancun Scenic Tower (Torre Escénica de Cancún), which you can take up for a panoramic view.

In the area right before the tower, there are a few theaters, a small church, and EL Embarcadero, an Ultramar dock with ferries to Isla Mujeres. Ferries leave about every hour between 9 a.m. and 5 p.m. and at the moment it's $19 USD.

In the other direction, across the bridge and on the right-hand side of the road, there's a small park with nice walking paths along the water. If you plan on walking all the way to Playa Tortuga or Playa Caracol, you can use these paths to avoid the sidewalk.

Another spot to catch an UltraMar ferry to Isla Mujeres is the Playa Tortuga ferry terminal, roughly halfway between El Embarcadero and Playa Caracol (where you can also catch the ferry). They all make a stop at El Embarcadero first, so for the most direct trip use that dock.

Ferries to Isla Mujeres from Playa Tortuga, Playa Caracol, or El Embarcadero are pricier than departing from Puerto Juárez north of downtown Cancun, but are obviously more convenient if you're staying in the hotel zone. (See **Other Places to Go** in the Appendix for information about Isla Mujeres.)

Playa Tortuga has shopping, a restaurant on the beach, and even a bungee jump at Adventure Bay next door, where you can arrange scuba diving, snorkeling, and other adventure tours.

Big Aquaworld, about halfway down the Zona Hotelera, also arranges all kinds of tours, including trips in a glass-bottom boat to the famous Underwater Museum of Art (Museo Subacuatico del Arte) off the southern tip of Isla Mujeres. Aquaworld is about a 10-minute walk north from the Mayan Museum.

A fun place to take your kids is the Wet 'n Wild Water Park in Ventura Park on the mainland near the airport, which also features swimming with dolphins.

Golfers will be happy that there are two clubs in the Zona Hotelera, the Cancun Golf Club at Pok ta Pok and the Iberostar Golf Club at the Hilton resort.

Some tequila museums are on the island, which seem to come and go with the tide—opening, closing, and reopening. You might learn some interesting facts about tequila, but remember that you can get a good bottle at a normal price from a supermarket downtown like Comercial Mexicana.

Finally, if you're into this sort of thing, many resorts will give you a free drink and a day pass to the swimming pools if you listen to one of their sales pitches. So if you see a resort that catches your fancy, ask at the front desk.

Tip: *If you are offered this deal—or a timeshare sales pitch—at some booth outside of the resort, or worse, by someone on the street, be wary of scams. Sure, listen if you're interested, but for no reason give them credit card numbers or any personal information, such as where you are staying in Cancun.*

4:30 pm -- Bus Back Downtown

- **Price:** MXN $10.50 (for a single adult)
- **Duration:** 30 minutes

To return to downtown Cancun, catch a bus marked "Centro" (downtown) going in the opposite direction from which you came. Keep your eyes open for when you enter downtown Cancun or ask to get let off near the bus terminal.

- *¿Nos podemos bajar por el terminal de ADO por favor?* Can we get off by the ADO terminal please?

5:00 pm -- Downtown Cancun

Downtown Cancun won't knock you out with its glamour or beauty, but behind busy streets are scenic parks, several markets, and lots of restaurants.

Tulum Av is Cancun's main drag. Bars, travel agencies, restaurants, and big supermarkets line the wide street. You can find banks with international ATMs between Av Uxmal (where the ADO terminal is) and Av Coba to the south.

Between Tulum Av and Yaxchilán Av, Parque las Palapas is a popular meeting point for locals and the best place for an inexpensive evening meal. You might even catch a free performance on its outdoor stage.

Walk down Yaxchilán Av to look for bars, restaurants, pool halls, and nightclubs. A few blocks away is Mercado 28.

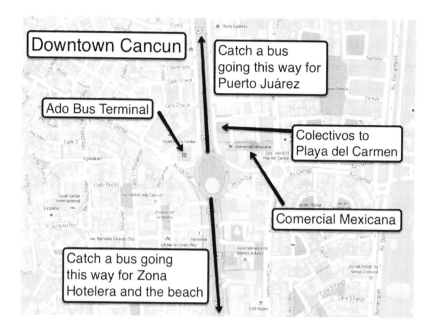

More Downtown

You can get a taste of Mexican suburbia by walking north on Tulum Av from the ADO terminal, where there's yet another market. After seven blocks, turn left on Cedro street to find Mercado 23, which is smaller but a lot less touristy than Mercado 28. Although souvenirs abound, you can also find fresh fruit, seafood, local cuisine, and a more authentic vibe.

Walk south on Tulum Av to see the city hall (Ayuntamiento) with the little plaza in front. The rest of Tulum Av is mostly fast food, small clothing shops, and convenience stores, though you might find an up-and-coming bar or restaurant. Look for a little pedestrian street on the other side of Tulum Av from city hall that leads back to Parque Las Palapas. Also, there are lots of discount hotel options as you continue farther south.

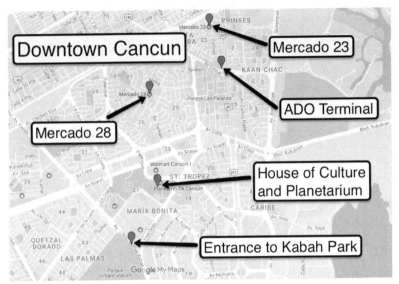

For a longer walk, after going south on Tulum Av, take a right on Coba Av to pass a few western-style malls. Then take your second left on Palenque St, pass the Walmart, and look for the Cancun House of Culture (Casa de la Cultura) in the park on your right, which provides information about performances and cultural events. Next door is the Ya'Kok Planetarium, and elsewhere in the park is the baseball stadium for the Quintana Roo Tigers and an Olympic/soccer stadium for Cancun's second division team, Atlante. South of the stadium is a bigger park, the Kabah Urban Park, full of walking trails in the jungle.

5:00 pm -- Walk to Mercado 28

- **Duration:** 15 minutes

Mercado 28 is a short walk from the ADO bus terminal.

Leave the terminal, walk across the parking lot, and go left on short Pino street. Then turn right on Uxmal Av. The next busy street is Yaxchilán, where you will take a left. Then after a few blocks take a right on Sunyaxchen Av. When the road splits, stay right and soon you will see a large parking lot and the entrance to the market on your left.

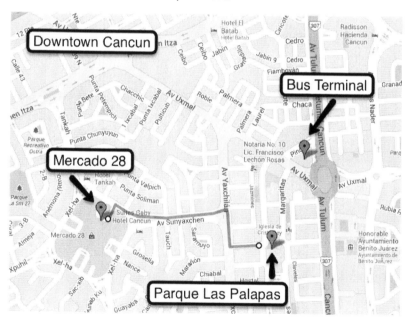

5:15 pm -- Mercado 28

- **Price:** FREE
- **Duration:** 1 hour
- **Address:** Av. Xel-Ha, Cancun Centro

Mercado 28 is perhaps the best place to buy souvenirs in Cancun. You'll see the same items in tourist destinations all over the Mayan Riviera, but here the prices get driven down because the market is far from the beach and so many vendors are all in one place.

But to get that good deal, expect to haggle. And get ready for every vendor you pass to call out to you as you walk by, maybe even giving you a funny nickname. They may seem aggressive, but this is just how they do business. (See **Money Matters** in the Appendix for haggling tips.)

If you're hungry, take a look at the little restaurants in the central part of the mall. Throughout Mexico, markets are a great place to get a late lunch. (Lunchtime in Mexico is between 2 and 4 p.m.) Prices are competitive and you can find local specialties. Many have set meals that include soup, rice, beans, a meat dish, and a drink for around 40 pesos. Look for a sign that says *comida corrida* or simply *comida*.

Tip: Trust the locals; always eat at the busiest restaurant in the market.

6:15 pm -- Walk to Parque Las Palapas

- **Duration:** 15 minutes

Parque las Palapas is a short walk from Mercado 28. Leave the market the way you came in, take a right, and walk down Sunyaxchen Av. Take a right on Yaxchilán, and then two blocks later take your next left. The park is a block ahead.

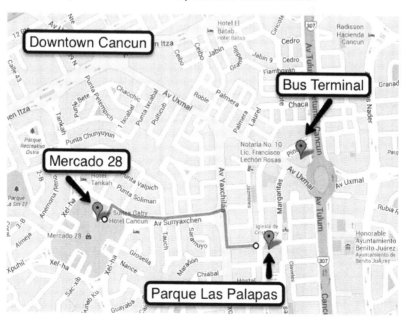

6:30 pm -- Parque Las Palapas

- **Price:** FREE
- **Duration:** 1 hour and 30 minutes
- **Address:** #31 Calle Margaritas, Cancun Centro

Parque las Palapas may have seen better days, but it's laid-back and spacious. Stroll through after dark while looking for a bar or restaurant in downtown Cancun and you may catch a free performance on the outdoor stage.

Besides that, the main reason to visit is to eat at the long row of outdoor food stalls. Take some time and look for something you'll like. You can get regional Yucatán food, like *salbutes* or *panuchos* (See **Food and Drink** in the Appendix for descriptions), or common Mexican favorites like tacos, tortas, *huaraches* (a long, flat tortilla with meat and cheese on top), or many other meat-tortilla-cheese variations. And for breakfast you can't beat a big fruit cocktail (*cóctel de fruta*).

8:00 pm -- Night Out in Cancun

- **Duration:** 3 hours and 50 minutes

If you want to hit a huge club, then head back to the Zona Hotelera. Many nightclubs have a fixed, all-you-can-drink entry fee. Most don't open until 10 or 11 and don't get going until after midnight.

The bus runs until 4 a.m. but becomes infrequent after midnight. Bring a card from your hotel (with its address) in case you need a cab later.

If that's not your scene or you're looking to save money, walk down Tulum Av or around Parque las Palapas. You can see a live salsa or rock band in a bar off the park or shoot pool onYaxchilán Av.

Extra Time in Cancun

Probably the best day trip from Cancun is to Isla Mujeres, where there's a nice village, good beaches, and excellent snorkeling and scuba diving, including at the famous Underwater Art Museum at the southern end of the island. Please see **Other Places to Go** in the Appendix for how to get to Isla Mujeres.

North of Cancun is Isla Blanca, which despite its name isn't an island but a long, undeveloped sandy peninsula. It's north of Puerto Juárez, where the ferries leave for Isla Mujeres, and without a rental car you'll have to negotiate a taxi and figure out how to get back to your hotel later. But if you go, you'll be rewarded with miles of sandy beach and clear water.

If you won't be staying in Playa del Carmen later, you can visit there on a day trip from Cancun. Catch a *colectivo* (passenger van) across the street from the ADO terminal downtown. In Playa del Carmen you can hop on another *colectivo* for Tulum and all points in between.

Halfway between Cancun and Playa del Carmen is the low-key beach town of Puerto Morelos, a great place to spend the day eating seafood and snorkeling. *Colectivos* and the ADO bus can take you there on their way to Playa del Carmen. If it drops you off on the side of the road, look for another *colectivo* nearby to take you into town—Puerto Morelos is about 10 minutes from the highway.

Besides enormous resorts, the coast from Cancun to Tulum is lined with adventure parks, *cenotes*, and other tourist attractions. Most are closer to Playa del Carmen than Cancun, and I describe those (the ones between Puerto Morelos and Tulum) in **Other Places to Go** in the Appendix. Below are two north of Puerto Morelos, so they are an easier day trip from Cancun than from Playa del Carmen.

Xochimilco Cancun is a reproduction of the famous canals and boat trips in Mexico City, where you'll drink tequila, listen to mariachis, and have a big feast. It's about five minutes south of the Cancun Airport.

Just north of Puerto Morelos, at the Croco Cun interactive zoo you and your kids can explore the jungle on a guided tour and touch many of the native animals.

You can take *colectivos* to and from these places, although if you take a taxi or rent a car you won't have to make the (sometimes) long walk from the highway to the entrance, which is especially important if you're traveling with children.

Day 2

============

Overview -- Valladolid

Valladolid's main claim to fame may be its proximity to Chichén Itzá, but its colonial architecture, authentic Mexican market, downtown *cenote*, 16th-century convent, and beautiful parks make it a great place for a short visit before going to the ruins.

This small town is worlds apart from the beach-going glitz of Cancun and Playa del Carmen. And by staying the night in Valladolid, you can have a head start on all the tour groups in Chichén Itzá the next day.

Named after the city in Spain, Valladolid was founded in 1543 by Francisco de Montejo, the nephew of the conquerer of the Yucatán, Francisco de Montejo. Originally located elsewhere on the peninsula, it was moved to its present site in 1545, built over ruins of a Mayan city called Zací. Yes, although the Mayan people still existed, the advanced Mayan civilization of Chichén Itzá and Tulum had already disappeared by the time the Spanish came to the New World.

During the Spanish colonial period Valladolid was the main point of development for the eastern Yucatán Peninsula and experienced a major uprising of the local Mayan population in 1848.

Like nearly every Mexican city, the exact center of Valladolid is the *zócalo*, or central park (*parque central*), officially known as the Parque Francisco Cantón, which is surrounded by hotels, restaurants, banks, government buildings, the cathedral, and the Bazar Municipal food court.

In all directions from the *zócalo*, Valladolid's narrow streets have more parks, museums, and churches—even a Buddhist temple. Take some time to wander around. If you're not up for too much walking, however, choose one direction: either toward the convent southwest of the *zócalo* or to the *cenote* and market to the northeast.

Valladolid can be a little confusing, with odd-numbered streets (*calles*) going east/west and even-numbered streets going north/south. If you ever get lost, just ask for the *zócalo*.

- *¿Disculpe, dónde está el zócalo?*
  Excuse me, where is the *zócalo*?

8:00 am -- Bus to Valladolid

- **Price:** MXN $206.00 (for a single adult)
- **Duration:** 2 hours and 30 minutes

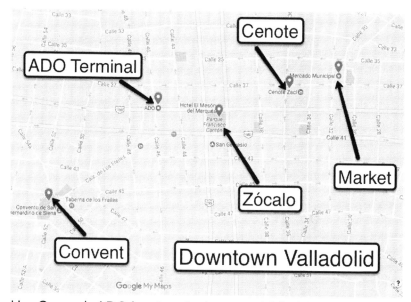

Use Cancun's ADO bus terminal to go to Valladolid. First- and second-class buses go there (and beyond to Chichén Itzá and Mérida), but when you ask for tickets they assume you want first class. There is little difference between them other than a possibly longer travel time from making more stops. So if you want to save money, ask for second class.

The first-class ADO bus takes between 2 and 2.5 hours, and costs 206 pesos. You can check schedules and fares on the ADO website.

If you haven't already checked online, then when you arrive at the Valladolid bus terminal, ask about the times for the bus to Playa del Carmen the following day. You will finish at Chichén Itzá sometime in the early afternoon, and it's good to have an idea of what time you'll need to be back in Valladolid to catch the bus.

See **Transportation** in the Appendix for instructions for checking schedules on the ADO website.

Note: The state of Yucatán (which contains Valladolid and Chichén Itzá) is in a different time zone than Cancun and Playa del Carmen in the state of Quintana Roo. When it's 10 o'clock in Quintana Roo, it's 9 in Yucatán, so plan accordingly when you travel between them. For the purposes of clarity I don't adjust for this on **Day 2** and **Day 3**, instead leaving the schedule in "real time."

10:30 am -- Get a Hotel in Valladolid

- **Duration:** 1 hour

Valladolid's *zócalo* is two blocks from the ADO terminal. Take a left on Calle 39 upon leaving the station.

There are many small hotels on and around the *zócalo*, including the Mesón de Marqués, a lovely old mansion located right next to the Bazar Municipal. It has a good restaurant in the central courtyard too.

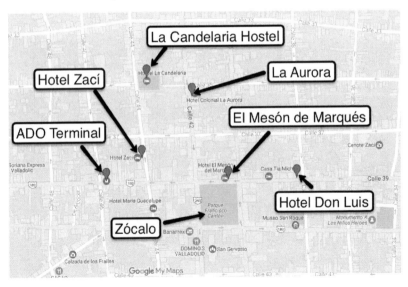

Here are four more clean, well-located, and reasonably-priced hotels. Look them up and check their reviews on booking.com:

- La Aurora Colonial is located on Calle 42 between Calles 35 and 37. It's on the higher end of budget hotels at 800-1,000 pesos a night, but it has a pool.
- Around the same price is Hotel Zací. It's on Calle 44 between Calles 37 and 39 and also has a pool.
- If you are looking for a something a little cheaper, for as low as 300 a night you can get a dorm bed in Hostal La Candelaria on Calle 35 between Calles 42 and 44 near Candelaria Park.
- A discount option with a pool, rooms at Hotel Don Luis cost between 300-500 pesos. It's on Calle 41 one block past the *zócalo* on the other side of the ADO terminal.

Some of the cheapest hotels in town are concentrated around the ADO terminal. These are quite basic and some aren't very clean. Just stop in to ask to see a room and for the prices, which may be posted behind the front desk.

11:30 am -- Walk to Bazar Municipal

- **Duration:** 10 minutes

The Bazar Municipal is on the *zócalo*. Take a left out of the bus terminal and walk three blocks down Calle 39.

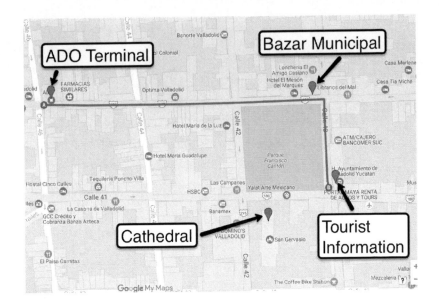

Look for the San Gervasio Cathedral on the other side of the *zócalo* from the Bazar, and if you have any questions, visit the tourist information center on the corner of Calles 40 and 41.

You can find international ATMs in the Bancomer and Banamex banks on the *zócalo*, and there's an HSBC ATM in the Bazar Municipal.

The tourist shops all around the *zócalo* lean more tasteful than in Cancun or Playa del Carmen, but remember that there is also a handicraft market near Cenote Zací. Wherever you go, if you don't see prices posted, get ready for some light haggling. See **Money Matters** in the Appendix for haggling tips.

11:40 am -- Brunch at Bazar Municipal

- **Duration:** 50 minutes

- **Address:** Calle 40 and Calle 39, Valladolid

Opposite the cathedral on the *zócalo*, this little food court sells Yucatán specialties, such as *panuchos* (a variation on tostadas) and puffy-tortilla *salbutes*. You can also find seafood and fresh juices.

Waiters yell and wave menus at potential patrons to choose their restaurant. Don't feel pressured—just look at the menu or move on. The *yucateca* food at each one is basically the same, with low prices, around 40 pesos a meal.

If you want something fancier, take a look at the Meson de Marques next door or any of the many restaurants on and around the *zócalo*, including Las Campanas and La Casona on Calle 41.

12:30 pm -- Walk to the San Roque Museum

- **Duration:** 10 minutes

The San Roque Museum, also known as the Valladolid Museum, is just around the corner from the *zócalo*. From the Bazar Municipal, walk down Calle 40 and take a left on Calle 41.

On the way you'll pass the Casa de Cultura (House of Culture), which is next to the tourist information center and may have free art or photography exhibits.

If you go straight on Calle 40 after Calle 41, you'll reach the **Casa de Los Venados**, a colonial home owned by an American expat couple with exhibitions of their collection of Mexican folk and contemporary art. It opens every day for tours at 10 a.m.

If you don't go to the museum and want a direct route to Cenote Zací, stay on Calle 39 after leaving the Bazar Municipal and then take a left on Calle 36.

12:40 pm -- San Roque Museum

- **Price:** FREE
- **Duration:** 1 hour
- **Address:** Calle 41 between Calles 38 and 40, Valladolid

The Museo Regional de San Roque has exhibits about the history of Valladolid, artifacts, and big murals. The building itself also has an interesting history: Founded in 1575, it has been a church, a hospital, and a convent.

The museum is free and open every day from 8 a.m. to 8 p.m.

1:40 pm -- Walk to Cenote Zací

- **Duration:** 20 minutes

The long way to the *cenote* takes you past a park with a monument to the child heroes of the Mexican Revolution, the picturesque Santa Ana church, and an artisanal market.

Turn left upon leaving the museum, walk two blocks until you take a left on Calle 34 (in front of the church), then take another left on Calle 39 and the next right on Calle 36.

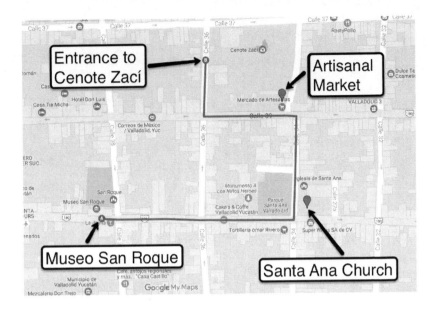

For the direct route, take a left on Calle 36 one block after leaving the museum.

Right after the museum you'll see La Joyita on the corner of Calles 41 and 38, which is a classic, old-style Mexican bar in a historic building. Another cool bar nearby with a lot of character is Don Trejo's *mezcalería*, where they specialize in mezcal, tequila's rustic cousin. From La Joyita take a right on Calle 38 and the next right on Calle 42.

On the corner of Calles 39 and 34, on the same block as the *cenote*, you'll see the thatched roof buildings of an artisanal market, an excellent place to browse for local crafts.

2:00 pm -- Cenote Zací

- **Price:** MXN $25.00 (for a single adult)
- **Duration:** 1 hour
- **Address:** Calle 37 between Calles 36 and 34, Valladolid

Cenote Zací may not have crystal-clear water like other, more famous cenotes, but you can swim in it. (Remember, on **Day 5** you will visit Dos Ojos Cenote, a *cenote* park in the jungle with swimming and scuba diving.) There are a few high ledges for big jumps and a little cave you can explore. It's a beautiful spot, especially impressive because of its convenient location in downtown Valladolid.

There is a restaurant on the site overlooking the *cenote*. Cenote Zací is open every day from 8 a.m. to 7 p.m.

3:00 pm -- Walk to the Municipal Market

- **Duration:** 10 minutes

Take a right out of the entrance to the *cenote* and take your first right on Calle 37. Walk two blocks until Calle 32 and look for the market on the left.

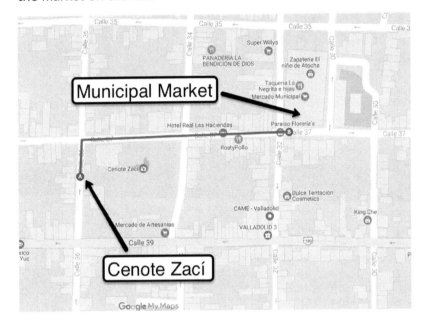

3:10 pm -- Municipal Market
- **Price:** FREE
- **Duration:** 50 minutes
- **Address:** Calle 32 and Calle 35, Valladolid

Valladolid's Municipal Market is just up the street from the *cenote*. This is a great place to buy fruit, vegetables, honey, and other fresh food for cheaper than in your next destination, Playa del Carmen. And of course, the market provides yet another opportunity to sample inexpensive, authentic local cuisine in its small restaurants and food stands.

Look for cacao seeds, the rawest chocolate.

Father and son selling yucca and honey products:

Tip: Always ask before photographing people. Mayans usually don't like having their picture taken, and doing it without permission is very rude. The easiest way to get permission is by buying something first.

4:00 pm -- Walk to the Convent

- **Duration:** 30 minutes

The gorgeous San Bernardino de Siena Convent is about as far away from the *zócalo* as the Municipal Market, but in the opposite direction. This location makes for pleasant wandering down the charming streets of Valladolid.

You can take the long way on Calle 35, which goes through scenic Candelaria Park with the Candelaria Church on the other side. There aren't many restaurants on this stretch, so if you're hungry (or want a direct route), turn left on Calle 40 or 42 to get back to the *zócalo*.

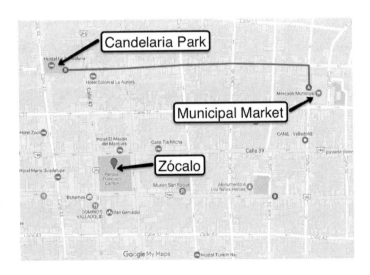

From Candelaria Park, you can either walk down scenic Calle 44 or past the *colectivo* station and bus terminal on Calle 46, as shown on the map below. Then turn right on the diagonal street Calzada de los Frailes, which begins at Calle 46 just past Calle 41. Look for the blue sign that says "San Bernardino de Sienna." A 5- or 10-minute walk on the narrow street takes you to pretty Sisal Park with the convent on the other side.

4:30 pm -- San Bernardino de Siena Convent

- **Price:** MXN $30.00 (for a single adult)
- **Duration:** 1 hour and 30 minutes
- **Address:** #238 Calle 49, Valladolid

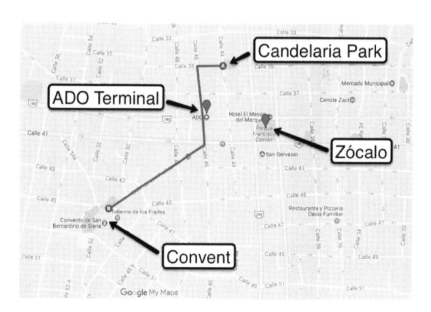

Built between 1552 and 1560, this Franciscan convent has a roomy chapel, a garden built over a *cenote*, and a small museum that describes its history. It's next to Sisal Park, an open, grassy area lined with pastel-painted shops and restaurants.

An especially good restaurant is the Taberna de los Frailes, where you can get Yucatán specialties, seafood, and craft beer. Look for it on the left-hand side of the convent.

The convent is open Monday to Saturday from 8 a.m. to 6 p.m. Wear long pants if you plan on visiting the church. Entry to the museum is 30 pesos. Outside the convent there is a light show in Spanish at 8 p.m. and another in English at 8:30, but expect this to change.

6:00 pm -- Valladolid by Night

- **Duration:** 1 hour

From the convent, you can walk back to the *zócalo* the same way you came on the diagonal Calzada de los Frailes or roam the side streets. Practically every block has historic buildings— some restored and some crumbling, some built from stacked stones and some in the Spanish-colonial style.

At night, the tree-filled *zócalo* and adjacent cathedral are bathed in colorful lights.

As you walk down Calle 41 while returning to the *zócalo* from the convent, you'll pass La Casona de Valladolid, a famous restaurant serving *yucateca* cuisine in an old mansion with a classic central courtyard. On the next block of Calle 41 look for the more modest restaurant Las Campanas, which besides authentic local food is a good place to get a beer.

If you have extra days in Valladolid, you can visit the *cenotes* Dzinup and Samula. They're on the same property on the way to Chichén Itzá and have a low entrance fee of 100 pesos. For more Mayan ruins, Ek Balam is a large site just 25 km (16 miles) north of Valladolid. And nature lovers should look into Rio Lagartos, a small town inside a huge biosphere reserve on the northern coast of the peninsula, which is famous for pink-water lagoons and lots of flamingos.

7:00 pm -- Chichén Itzá Night Show

- **Price:** MXN $450.00 (for a single adult)
- **Duration:** 2 hours

If you can't wait for tomorrow to see Chichén Itzá, then you can go in the evening for the Noches de Kukulkán light and sound show (*luz y sonido*). Loud, dramatic voices narrate the history of the ancient city in Spanish while the Castillo pyramid is lit up in deep colors.

The starting time for the night show is between 6:30 and 7 p.m., depending on when the sun sets. The current price is 450 pesos, but expect this to change.

In fact, from time to time the show is free, so take a look at the night show website (only in Spanish). But for more reliable up-to-date information, it's better to ask locals, like at your hotel, the *colectivo* station, or the tourist information center on the *zócalo*.

You can take a *colectivo* to the ruins in the evening (See **Day 3**), but returning to Valladolid from Chichén Itzá at night isn't so simple. Unless there are taxis waiting and you don't mind paying for the 40-minute trip (remember to negotiate beforehand), you'll have to walk out to the highway, stand on the side of the road, and flag down a bus coming from Mérida. Take a left on the highway from the road leaving the ruins, and don't cross the road, but wait on that same side.

This part of Mexico is generally safe, but if you're nervous, walk up the road to a small police checkpoint. It's easier to catch the bus there too because it will slow down to roll over the checkpoint speedbump.

Day 3
============

Overview -- Chichén Itzá

On this day, you spend the morning in Chichén Itzá and the afternoon on a bus to Playa del Carmen. Buses from Valladolid to Playa del Carmen are less frequent than to Cancun, so be sure to look up the schedule online or ask at the ADO bus terminal as soon as possible so you can plan your day.

At the time of writing, there's only one afternoon bus direct from Chichén Itzá to Playa del Carmen. If you want to take this bus, then bring your luggage to the ruins. There's a free left luggage service there.

If not, then leave your bags behind the front desk of your hotel in Valladolid. You can have lunch in Valladolid before you leave for Playa del Carmen.

7:00 am -- Colectivo to Chichén Itzá

- **Price:** MXN $80.00 (for a single adult)
- **Duration:** 1 hour

Colectivos(passenger vans) to Chichén Itzá leave more frequently than the ADO bus. You don't make reservations or buy advance tickets, just show up when you're ready to go.

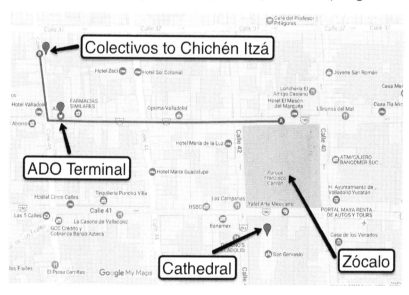

Chichén Itzá opens at 8 a.m., and if you plan on arriving then, please visit the*colectivo* station in Valladolid beforehand to confirm the price and earliest departure times, as they tend to change.

At the time of writing *colectivos* charge 80 pesos and the ADO bus is 94 pesos. The trip by bus is about 50 minutes and the *colectivo* takes about 40. So, combined with walking to the station and waiting for the van to fill with passengers so it can leave, plan on spending an hour getting to Chichén Itzá.

Note: If you drive from Cancun or Playa del Carmen, be aware that Valladolid and Chichén Itzá are in a different time zone, which is one hour earlier. So if you leave Cancun at 6 a.m., you will arrive in Chichén Itzá around 8, shaving an hour off the nearly three-hour trip. Playa del Carmen is a little more than two hours from Chichén Itzá. Also, if you drive, bring cash for tolls, at least 300 pesos each way.

Driving into Valladolid after visiting Chichén Itzá is easy—after the ruins, take a right on the highway and drive straight to the zócalo, around which there are several parking lots if you can't find a spot on the street.

8:00 am -- The Mayan Ruins of Chichén Itzá

- **Price:** MXN $232.00 (for a single adult)
- **Duration:** 7 hours

Chichén Itzá is only a few hours from Cancun, but the ancient Mayan city with its pyramids, skull carvings, and two *cenotes* will give you a taste of the history of the region that you certainly wouldn't get if you only stayed on the beach.

Many people go to Chichén Itzá as part of a large, loud, rushed tour group, but getting there on your own is easy. Doing it in a day trip from Cancun is possible, but this would be a very long day. Staying in the town of Valladolid the night before puts you in a great position to have all day to see the large complex and get there in the morning before it gets crowded.

In high season, even if you arrive before 8 a.m. when it opens, there might already be a big line of people waiting for tickets. In low season, however, you can probably get your tickets and walk right in without waiting.

Chichén Itzá is famous for El Castillo (the castle), aka the Pyramid of Kukulkán, the blocky, angular pyramid built to represent the Mayan calendar (for example, 91 steps on four sides, or 364, plus the platform, 365). The time of its construction is estimated to be between 650 and 800 AD.

You'll see tour groups clapping on one side of the pyramid. Go to over there and try it for yourself. The perfection of the layout and the surrounding architecture makes the sound bounce off three structures and come back to you as a sharp, squeaky noise.

Near El Castillo is the largest ball court in the Mayan world, with high goals on either side, platforms for royal spectators, and lots of intricate carvings.

From here you can walk down a vendor-lined path to the Sacred Cenote, where there is also a small building with snacks, cold drinks, ice cream, and bathrooms.

Opposite the ball court from El Castillo is the Thousand Columns Group, with the Market (also full of columns) and the smaller Xtoloc Cenote beyond. Keep going down the path to check out some of the most interesting buildings in the whole city around the Church just past the Observatory.

Going on your own means you won't have a tour guide explaining everything to you. While the site can be appreciated for its beauty alone, if you want to know the significance of what you are seeing, hire a guide or buy a guidebook from the gift shop.

Tip: *If you are really cheap, eavesdrop on tour groups. Many are in English.*

To enterChichén Itzá, first you get in line for a ticket and then give it to someone at the gate, which is beyond the ticket window on the other side of the bookstore.

You might see shorter lines, but don't get in one unless you're sure it's for the regular tickets. The other lines might be for tour groups (there's a separate window for groups of 15 or more) or Mexican students, teachers, and pensioners, who get in free here and at most ruins and museums in Mexico.

The total price for foreigners is 232 pesos, 167 of which goes to the state and 65 to the federal government. For Mexicans it is 154 pesos (89 state and 65 federal) and free on Sunday.

If you bring a video camera, you'll have to pay 45 pesos at another window. Ask when you pay for the ticket. Also, the free left-luggage area is next to the bathrooms.

Unless you pack a lunch or some snacks, your only option is the overpriced restaurant at the entrance. If you can wait, it's better to eat lunch back in Valladolid before you head off to Playa del Carmen.

Chichén Itzá is open from 8 a.m. to 5 p.m., with the last visitors admitted at 4 p.m.

Note: You may have noticed that this itinerary allocates seven hours for Chichén Itzá. While you could easily spend that much time at the site, you could also use a few of these hours for lunch and a little more exploring in Valladolid before getting on the bus to Playa del Carmen. A good idea would be to buy your bus tickets for Playa del Carmen at the ADO terminal in the morning or the day before, and then after you visit Chichén Itzá, spend a few more hours in town before the bus leaves.

3:00 pm -- Colectivo and Bus to Playa del Carmen

- **Price:** MXN $206.00 (for a single adult)
- **Duration:** 4 hours

From Chichén Itzá, take a *colectivo* or an ADO bus back to Valladolid and then another ADO bus to Playa del Carmen. Check out of your hotel and leave your bags behind the front desk in the morning before you go to the ruins.

Chichén Itzá to Valladolid by *colectivo* takes about 40 minutes, and then the bus from Valladolid to Playa del Carmen takes about 2.5 hours. Buses leave every hour or two. Check travel times on the ADO website or ask at the terminal, because some buses between Valladolid and Playa del Carmen take about 40 minutes more because they go the long way with a stop in Tulum.

All in all, expect the trip to take about four hours, including walking between terminals and waiting for departures.

Another option is to go straight from the ruins to Playa del Carmen. You can leave your luggage for free by the bathrooms at the front gate. At the time of writing, there is only one afternoon bus direct from Chichén Itzá to Playa del Carmen, which costs 184 to 206 pesos. Itdeparts at 4:30 p.m. and takes about 3.5 hours. Confirm this on the website or at the ADO terminal in Valladolid.

If you miss every bus and don't want to stay another night in Valladolid, go back to Cancun and from there take a *colectivo* to Playa del Carmen. They depart from Pino St in front of the ADO terminal downtown, or across Tulum Av in the parking lot next to Comercial Mexicana, and run late, usually until midnight.

Playa del Carmen has two bus stations. The main one is on Quinta Av, the pedestrian street that follows the beach. You'll probably arrive here, but there's a chance you end up at the second one. If so, just ask the way to Quinta Avenida (pronounced *KEEN-ta a-ve-NI-da*).

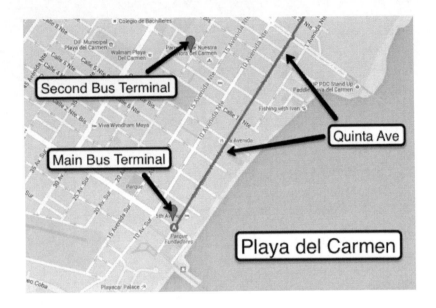

7:00 pm -- Walk to Hotels in Playa del Carmen

- **Duration:** 1 hour
- **Address:** ADO Terminal: Av. Juárez and Quinta Ave., Col Centro, Playa del Carmen, Quintana Roo

Playa del Carmen has hundreds of hotels and hostels for any budget: fancybeachside resorts, stylish guesthouses, party hostels, and no-frills cheapies.

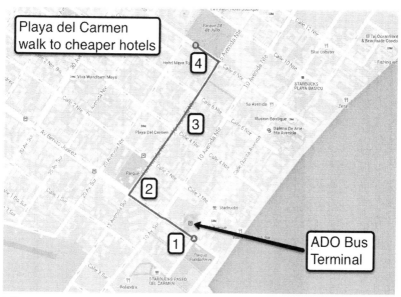

Like for downtown Cancun, it's easy to arrive without reservations and walk around looking at hotels. In the low season you should have no problem finding a room, but in the high season many places will be booked, especially if you arrive in the late afternoon. (See **When to Go** in the Appendix for high and low season dates.) You'll have a better chance of finding a room in the morning, but you'll have to wait until 12-2 p.m. for them to clean it. To make reservations, check their websites for rates and contact information, or search for hotels on booking.com, tripadvisor.com, or any travel website you like.

The best (and most expensive) hotels are between Quinta Av and the beach. Especially in the low season, you can find good value there, not to mention luxury and the sounds of waves at night. Just walk down Quinta Av or the beach and ask at the lobby. People speak English at these hotels.

Below are two other walks to find hotels in Playa del Carmen. To look for budget hotels, take a right out of the ADO bus terminal and then another right on Benito Juárez St, and walk two blocks up. There are five budget and mid-range hotels on this stretch. Then take a right on 15 Av, and for the next four blocks you'll pass more than 10 hotels and hostels. Below are my recommendations. Please remember that prices are bound to change:

1. Posada Lily: No other hotel in Playa is this cheap and this close to both the beach and the ADO bus terminal. 350 pesos for a double or single in the low and high seasons. And it's clean!
2. This block of 15 Av across the street from the park full of food stands has extra-cheap hotels, some with kitchens, some with air conditioning, and some not so clean. Their names are: Paso del Mar, Hotel Colores Mexicanos, and Hotel Quiam.
3. Hotel Atlantida gets my recommendation for a slightly-more-than-cheap choice because of its spacious, clean rooms, many balconies, and friendly staff. 500 pesos for a single and 600 for a double in low season, 700 for a single and 900 for a double in high season.
4. If you still can't find something to your taste and budget, take a left on Calle 8 when you reach the big park for a few more discount hotels. For more mid-range hotels, look on Calle 4, Calle 6, and Calle 8 in the direction of the beach.

Walk up 10 Av instead of 15 Av if you want something nicer and don't mind spending a little more money, such as between 1,000-1,500 pesos. Here and on side streets are many hotels with decent prices and local style.

I can highly recommend Hotel Barrio Latino, which is on Calle 4 between 10 and 15 Av. It's a small yet clean and quiet place with helpful staff and reasonable rates (about 1,000 pesos regular season). And you can't beat the location.

Finally, although it's not on the beach, and actually quite expensive at $230 USD per night for the most basic room, La Tortuga is a beautiful place with a jacuzzi, pool table, nice bar, and lots of trees. And it's out of earshot of the nightclubs.

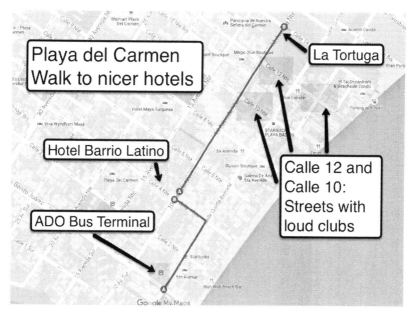

Tip: *Be warned that Calle 10 and Calle 12 between 10 Av and the beach have really loud nightclubs, which might make sleeping difficult, if in fact sleep is what you're looking for. Things seem calm in the daytime, but after midnight...*

8:00 pm -- Quinta Avenida—Fifth Ave

- **Duration:** 3 hours

Walk down Quinta Av, the main drag in Playa del Carmen, which follows the beach. Day and night, restaurants serve pizza, burgers, and bland tacos. (Mexicans tend to think that foreigners, especially Americans, don't like spicy food.) Waiters wave menus in your face, and hawkers offer cheap souvenirs, jewelry, and t-shirts. Looming behind are three fancy shopping malls, one at the southern end of Quinta Av, one on Calle 12, and another on Constituyentes.

The souvenirs are overpriced and you can find more authentic Mexican food elsewhere, but still Quinta Av makes for a great evening stroll. Check out all the tourists, party people, mariachis, and hustlers.

Unless you want foreign food or happy hour drinks, I recommend searching out a real Mexican restaurant a little farther inland. If the menu is painted on the wall and there aren't any nachos on the table, you should pay half price and eat twice as well. (See **Some Dining Suggestions** on **Day 4**.)

Day 4

============

8:00 am -- Playa del Carmen

- **Duration:** 4 hours

Finally, a whole day on the beach. No bus rides. No hotel check-in.

Playa del Carmen (often shortened to Playa, which means *beach*) is about an hour south of Cancun. While Cancun's beach is in the shadow of massive resorts, Playa's sky-blue Caribbean water and white-sand beachfront is lined with a mix of restaurants and small hotels, none higher than four or five stories. Quinta Av (Fifth Ave), a pedestrian-only street of hotels, shops, and restaurants, follows the beach. You'll never need to take a taxi in Playa del Carmen.

After Quinta Av, going away from the beach, the streets get numbered by adding five: 10 Av, 15 Av, 20 Av, and so forth. 10 Av has mid-range and luxury hotels, plenty of cool bars, and smaller restaurants. 15 Av has budget hotels, a few parks, and more authentic Mexican food. If you like to walk, explore both to see what's up.

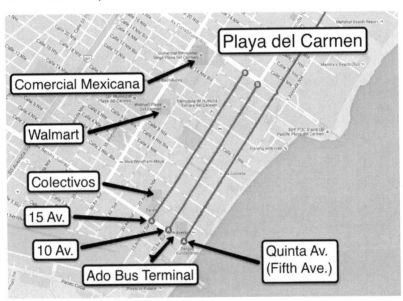

Running perpendicular to the avenidas are the calles. The major street that leads to the ADO bus terminal is Benito Juárez. Could it be considered Calle Zero? Going north from there, the calles are all even numbers: Calle 2, Calle 4, Calle 6, and onward.

The next major street going perpendicular to the beach, after Calle 18, is Constituyentes. Walk toward the sea to go out on a pier and turn north for Mamitas beach, which has more space than the main beach. Walk away from the sea on Constituyentes to find some good taco restaurants and Comercial Mexicana.

Tip: Comercial Mexicana is a huge superstore, and there's a Walmart a few blocks south. Go there for groceries, clothes, and tequila. Don't buy tequila in a souvenir shop on Quinta Av, as it will be insanely overpriced (though they do give free samples).

Playa Mamitas

After crossing Constituyentes, Quinta Av continues as a pedestrian street for two more kilometers, though after Calle 34 cars can enter it to parallel park.

Colectivos to Tulum, Cancun, and all points in between leave from Calle 2 between 15 and 20 Av. See **Transportation** and **Other Places to Go** in the Appendix for more information.

Don't use the ATMs on Quinta Av, as they charge higher fees than bank ATMs. Look for several banks (Banamex, Santander, Bancomer) on Benito Juárez near 25 Av, or go the Bannorte on 10 Av between Calle 8 and Calle 10 or the Scotiabank on 10 Av and Constituyentes. There's also an international Bancomer ATM in the ADO terminal.

If you arrive in Playa some other way than the bus, like by car or in a *colectivo*, you might not even notice the ADO terminal among all the souvenir shops, pizza-slice storefronts, and drink-mixing stands. Look for it kitty-corner from the church on Quinta Av and Benito Juárez St.

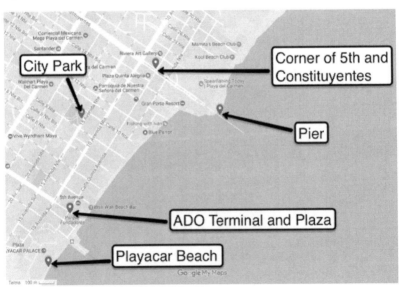

If the main beach is too crowded, walk 10 minutes in either direction to get more space on Mamitas beach to the north of the pier at the end of Constituyentes, or Playacar beach south of the Cozumel dock. Walk through Señor Frogs to get to Playacar beach—they don't mind.

Tip: Unlike other parts of Mexico, public drinking is unofficially allowed in Playa del Carmen. Walking down Quinta Av with a beer in your hand is no problem. If you want to save money, buy a caguama, a 40 ounce-ish size bottle at OXXO or any convenience store. You pay a deposit, so save the receipt for when you return the bottle. But watch out—you can't buy alcohol from a store on Sunday afternoon.

12:00 pm -- Walk to Bird Sanctuary

- **Duration:** 20 minutes

The Xaman-Ha Bird Sanctuary is located inside the fancy gated community Playacar. It's a pleasant 10- or 15-minute walk from the ADO terminal. Go south on 10 Av past the big shopping mall to the Playacar gates. Keep to the left at the roundabout and walk straight on Paseo Xaman-Ha. You'll see the entrance to the bird sanctuary on your right.

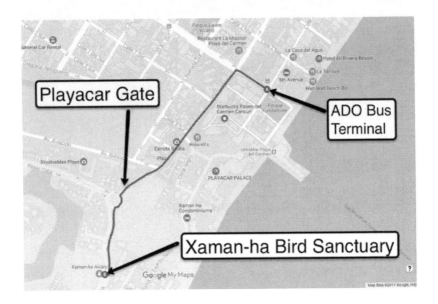

12:20 pm -- Xaman-Ha Bird Sanctuary

- **Price:** MXN $300.00 (for a single adult)
- **Duration:** 1 hour and 20 minutes
- **Address:** Paseo Xaman-Ha, Manzana 13-A Lote 1, Fraccionamiento Playacar

The Xaman-Ha Bird Sanctuary (Aviario Xaman-Ha) is a small place, and if you walk quickly you can get through it in about 15 minutes. At 300 pesos the entrance fee may seem a little steep, but it's necessary for maintaining this beautiful natural refuge that has survived for 23 years among all the condos and timeshares with astronomical property values.

But slow down and take a seat on a bench, and you can observe the birds and other animals eating, drinking, and doing their thing. Other than a small covered area that you can walk through, the bird sanctuary is open—the birds are free to come and go as they please.

Aside from macaws, parrots, flamingos, and lovely native birds you haven't yet heard of, you'll see iguanas, the jungle rodent *sereque* (AKA agouti or guaqueque, depending on which Mayan dialect is being spoken), and, if you're lucky, a spider monkey high in the trees. These solitary monkeys venture in from the jungle for a day or two to steal some fruit and then move on.

The bird sanctuary is open every day from 9 a.m. to 5 p.m. Children under 12 get in free. Don't forget a bottle of water and your camera.

1:40 pm -- Walk Back to Quinta Av

- **Duration:** 20 minutes

Walk back to Quinta Av the way you came. From the bird sanctuary, take a left on Paseo Xaman-Ha, walk through the Playacar gate, and then go down 10 Av.

Or, if you're up for more walking, you can visit some Mayan ruins just down the road. Walk for about 10 minutes on Paseo Xaman-Ha in the opposite direction from the Playacar gate to find the Xaman-Ha ruins, also known as the Playacar ruins. Entrance is free. From the ruins you could then walk toward the sea and look for a path between timeshares to the beach.

Note: Xaman-Ha, by the way, was the name of the Mayan city where Playa del Carmen is now located.

2:00 pm -- Shopping on Quinta Av

- **Duration:** 2 hours

Yes, there are no fewer than three full-sized, Western-style malls on Quinta Av with all the name brands you'd expect. And, although you'll see souvenir shops everywhere, for efficient comparison shopping go to the concentration of small stores at the southern end of Quinta Av after the ADO terminal.

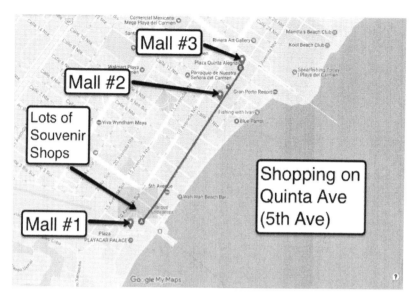

As you surely have noticed, tour guides and souvenir salesman constantly call out to you as you walk by. You only need one word: *gracias* (thank you), which also means *no thank you*. Don't hesitate to look at something, accept a free sample, ask questions, or ask for the price. But if you don't want it, don't be apologetic, and try not to feel pressured. Just smile and give a firm *gracias*, and walk away.

Talk to the tour guides if you want, but you don't need them to book anything unless it's out of the ordinary. If you want to go snorkeling or diving, visit a dive shop. To go to Cozumel, Isla Mujeres, or nearby beaches, do it on public transportation, and buy your tickets directly at the ferry terminal or at the *colectivos*. And to go to the heavily advertised adventure parks with funny names like Xel-Ha, Xcaret, Xplor, etc., you can buy tickets online and then take a *colectivo* there.

Tip: *Restaurants, souvenir shops, and tour guides often quote prices in U.S. dollars. Unless it's a fixed price, like at a nightclub or on an ecopark website, you're much better off paying in pesos, as the exchange rate they give you for dollars will be outrageous.*

4:00 pm -- Papantla Flyers and Other Entertainment

- **Price:** FREE
- **Duration:** 2 hours

Spacious Parque Fundadores between the ADO terminal and the dock for ferries to Cozumel has a lot going on. Sometimes a wedding party gathers at the church, called La Capilla de Nuestra Señora del Carmen (Our Lady of Carmen Chapel).

In the little plaza next to the church, Los Voladores de Papantla (Papantla Flyers) do their show several times a day. Originally from Veracruz, this performance can be seen throughout Mexico. At the end, they'll pass around a tip jar—toss in 10 pesos (at least):

You can take your kids (or yourself on a rainy day) to the **3D Museum of Wonders** on 10 Av and Calle 8, open from 9 a.m. to 10 p.m. daily; or to **L'Aquarium Playa del Carmen** on Quinta Av and Calle 14, open Mon-Fri 12 p.m. to 9 p.m, Sat-Sun 10 a.m. to 10 p.m.

It's fun to explore Playa by bicycle. Several shops rent cruiser bikes by the day, including Muscaria Car Rental on 10 Av between Calles 6 and 8. There's a bike lane on 10 Av until Constituyentes, and after Calle 30 you can ride on Quinta Av.

Finally, if you don't want to sit on the beach and have already explored Quinta Av, then think about taking the ferry to Cozumel for the day. You can't miss the ferry terminal on the southern end of the main beach, and several ferry companies leave all day, every day. The cheapest is Ultramar, and at the time of writing a return ticket is 140 pesos.

But besides Cozumel, the Caribbean coast on both sides of Playa del Carmen is full of smaller towns, beaches, *cenotes*, and ecoparks, all easily accessible by *colectivo* or taxi. Playa's location roughly halfway between Cancun and Tulum makes it a great base for day trips. Please see **Other Places to Go** in the Appendix for a summary of these places and tips for Cozumel.

6:00 pm -- Dining in Playa

- **Duration:** 3 hours

Wandering down Quinta Av is the easiest way to find a restaurant. You can find good Italian, good Falafel, good grilled sausages, and much more. Fine dining abounds, especially a few blocks north of Constituyentes. Expect higher prices in fancy spots, although you may find them cheaper than comparable restaurants back home.

But for real Mexican food or regional food from the Yucatán, skip the places on Quinta Av, as they tend to sell "Americanized" Mexican food, with bland salsas and inflated prices. Sure, these restaurants are conveniently located and serve tasty margaritas, but in general you're much better off venturing a few blocks inland to sample the authentic (and cheap).

Many inexpensive restaurants that serve regional or Mexican food are concentrated around 15 Av and Calle 4, including a small restaurant that serves *tlayudas* from the state of Oaxaca and several that specialize in *tortas*, Mexican sandwiches.

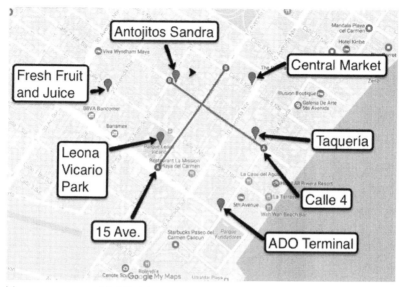

Here are some highlights:

- Leona Vicario Park on Benito Juárez and 15 Av has a bunch of taco stands: cheap, fast, and real. It has souvenir and jewelry vendors too.
- Antojitos Sandra is a locals' favorite for Yucatán finger food like *panuchos, salbutes,* and *polcanes.* (See**Food and Drink**in the Appendix for descriptions.) It's on Calle 4 almost on the corner with 20 Av, and there's a shrimp and fish taco spot across the street.
- Taqueria la Riviera Costeña is an excellent place to try authentic *tacos al pastor*, which come from the big red spit of meat outside. A plate of five is 100 pesos—a little more expensive than usual, but a good deal for a restaurant only one block from the beach.

- The local restaurants with outdoor seating in the Playa del Carmen Central Market on Calle 6 and 10 Av are popular, casual, and highly affordable—check them out for breakfast too.
- There's a busy corner spot on 25 Av and Calle 2 that sells fresh juice and fruit cocktails. You'll also see fresh juices for sale near the *colectivos* on Calle 2.

Besides local food, Calle 4 is a good street to look for modest-yet-quality foreign establishments, with Falafel, an Italian coffeeshop, and a German beer garden.

Also, check out Constituyentes for authentic food. From Quinta Av., walk toward the sea to find Aguachiles, which serves excellent Mexican-style seafood and *caguamas*, big bottles of beer. In the other direction, away from the beach, there are several taco restaurants across the street from

Comercial Mexicana. El Fogon is the most popular. Ask for *tacos al pastor*, the marinated pork on the big vertical spit, like a Mexican shawarma.

9:00 pm -- Night Out in Playa Del Carmen

- **Duration:** 2 hours and 55 minutes

By night, Quinta Av is filled with music, a good indicator of what type of bar or club to expect. Many clubs are on Calle 10 and Calle 12.

The big, fancy dance clubs on Calle 12 have high covers, all-you-can-drink open bars, and international DJs. Smaller bars and clubs on Calle 10, 10 Av, and Quinta Av have reasonable or no covers and local DJs spinning current hits. There are no dress codes in Playa.

Go toward the beach on Calle 12 for the most popular and most expensive clubs like the **Blue Parrot** on the beach (40-60 USD cover), **Mandala**, **Abolengo**, **Palazzo**, and **La Vaquita**.

Coco Bongo is promoted all over Quinta Av. With live shows featuring acrobats and celebrity impersonators, it's like a Vegas show inside a nightclub. The cover is between 50-60 USD and includes an open bar.

There are more clubs and bars one block over on Calle 10, including **L'Ambassade**, a cheap bar with no cover where you can order a huge mojito and look out from the second floor at the chaos on the street below.

If you want to dance salsa, look for **Danzantes** (Calle 12) or the Cuban restaurant-bar **La Bodeguita del Medio**, located on Quinta Av and Calle 36. Also, **Zenzi** on the beach has Latin and many other types of live music.

Several sports bars are on and near Quinta Av, including well-priced **La Taberna** on 10 Av and Calle 4. And for something different, you can sing karaoke on Calle 6 between Quinta and 10 Av.

Prices change and clubs go in and out of fashion, so the best way to choose a nightspot is to just walk around, listen to the music, and look at the people coming and going. Or you can check out their websites and Facebook pages for the latest updates.

Tip: *In some clubs in Playa or Cancun, if you are a girl or with a group of girls, you may not have to pay cover. Smile at the doorman and ask to be let in for free—but please don't feel bad if he says no.*

Day 5

============

Overview -- Tulum

Tulum is about an hour south of Playa del Carmen. Tulum can refer to three distinct places, all a few km apart: the Mayan ruins, the beach, and the small highway town. The ruins are some of the most beautiful in Mexico, mainly because of their location on cliffs overlooking the sky-blue Caribbean.

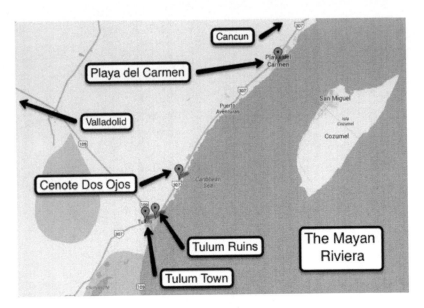

Dos Ojos Cenote is on the way to Tulum, making for an easy one- or two-hour stop on your way to the ruins. Bring a swimsuit, towel, sunscreen, sunglasses, and a camera. Wait until after the *cenote* to put on your sunscreen because it's bad for the fresh water. You'll be walking around outside a lot, so you may want to bring a hat to protect yourself from the sun.

You can eat lunch outside the Tulum ruins, and unless you want to venture into Tulum town (10 minutes down the road in a *colectivo* or taxi), the few small (but decent) restaurants there are your only option. So think about preparing a lunch in Playa del Carmen. Buy a sandwich from Comercial Mexicana, or better yet, get some *empanadas* at one of the little restaurants on Calle 2 between Quinta Av and the *colectivos*. At least bring a few liters of water because you'll spend the day swimming and walking around in the sun.

Tip: *If you go during high season, you may want to go to the ruins before the* cenote, *as the ruins can get quite crowded.*

9:00 am -- Colectivo to Dos Ojos Cenote

- **Price:** MXN $30.00 (for a single adult)
- **Duration:** 30 minutes

Take a *colectivo* to Dos Ojos Cenote. Make sure the driver knows that you will get off there, not Tulum.

From the ADO bus terminal, walk down Quinta Av and take a left on Calle 2. After 15 Avyou'll see a line of people waiting on the sidewalk across from the park. (For*colectivos*to Cancun, walk to the end ofthe block, just before 20 Av.)

The minimum price for the *colectivo* is 20 pesos, and it's 40 to the Tulum ruins. They should charge 30 for Dos Ojos Cenote.

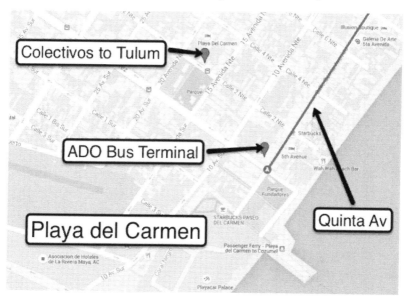

Tip: *The* colectivo *driver's helper will ask your destination before you get in. If you're going to Tulum or Cancun, don't worry about it, but if your destination is something less common, like Dos Ojos*

Cenote or Xpu-ha beach, pay attention to the signs on the highway in case the driver forgets. And unless the driver asks, wait to pay until the end when you get out.

9:30 am -- Dos Ojos Cenote

- **Price:** MXN $200.00 (for a single adult)
- **Duration:** 2 hours and 30 minutes
- **Address:** Carr. Fed. 307 Tulum-Playa del Carmen

The Yucatán peninsula is basically a huge flat sponge of limestone covered with jungle. A vast network of underground rivers and caves holds fresh water, essential to the inhabitants of the region. Where you have access to this network—a big sinkhole or cavern—you have a *cenote*, a great place to swim and explore.

There are plenty of *cenotes* near Tulum, but Dos Ojos is one of the largest, most reasonably priced, and most conveniently located.

The *cenote* is about a 20-minute walk through the jungle from the entrance on the side of the highway. The guys at the gate will try to get you to take a taxi, but there's no reason why you can't walk. They will also try to get you to buy a package that may include a guide, snorkel gear, or scuba gear. You can wait until you are at the *cenote* to rent anything, and a guide is not necessary unless you'll be scuba diving.

Cenote Dos Ojos is open from 8 a.m. to 5 p.m. every day of the week. Renting a snorkel and goggles costs 30 pesos, with another 30 pesos for flippers.

Tip: If you're coming from Playa del Carmen, only want to visit a cenote, *and won't goto Tulum on the same trip,* go to Cenote Cristiliano or one of the other three cenotes just south of Playa del Carmen. They're a lot closer than Dos Ojos but are similarly beautiful, inexpensive, and low-key. See **Other Places to Go** in the Appendix for more information.

12:00 pm -- Colectivo to Tulum

- **Price:** MXN $20.00 (for a single adult)
- **Duration:** 20 minutes

Walk back the way you came, stand by the highway, and flag down any white van that looks like a *colectivo*. Don't worry if one passes you. It might be a private charter, and another is bound to pass soon. Tell them to take you to the Tulum ruins—*las ruinas de Tulum.*

The *colectivo* may turn on the road to the ruins or let you off on the highway. The way to the ruins is clearly marked. It's about a 10-minute walk from the highway to the entrance. There's no need to buy anything from the tourist stands on the way. You can buy your ticket for the ruins right before you enter.

Tulum is open every day from 8 a.m. to 5 p.m., with the last people admitted at 4:30 p.m. Entrance costs 70 pesos, and you can check for updates on the page for Tulum on the website for the Mexican Secretary of Culture. It's in Spanish but times and prices should be obvious.

If you didn't bring a lunch, then you can eat at one of the little restaurants on the way to the ruins. The prices may be a little higher (between 50-200 pesos) than a similar restaurant in Tulum town or Playa del Carmen, but the food is tasty with lots of seafood options.

12:20 pm -- The Mayan Ruins of Tulum

- **Price:** MXN $70.00 (for a single adult)
- **Duration:** 4 hours and 40 minutes

The ancient Mayan ruins of Tulum are built on cliffs over the sea. Interesting limestone structures are scattered throughout the grassy compound where huge iguanas sun themselves.

Don't miss the little beach under the tallest structure, El Castillo (the castle), also known as the lighthouse. Despite its tiny size, it's one of the most famous beaches in Mexico, routinely appearing on "Top X Best Beaches" lists. Swimming out in the gentle waves, turning around, and looking at the ruins from the water may impress you even more than gazing up at Chichén Itzá's iconic pyramid.

Tulum the beach (not the little one under the ruins) is a 20-minute walk farther south. Skip it if you're tired of walking or don't want to pay for a cab later. But if you want to go and have the time, then after leaving the

ruins, take a left and then follow the road until it reaches the beach. There are no services on the beach, but it is wide and pristine.

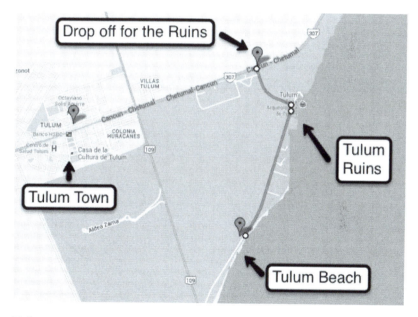

Tulum town is a long, hot walk (at least an hour) from the beach, though it's easy to wave down a taxi. The town seems like little more than a tourist stopover until after dark, when locals hang around the basketball courts eating street food and neon bars serve up fish, beer, and loud party music. If you have more time, you can find decent, well-priced hotels in Tulum town, which is a good base for exploring more *cenotes* (look for Gran Cenote) or the Mayan ruins of Cobá farther inland and deep in the jungle. (See **Other Places to Go** in the Appendix.)

5:00 pm -- Return to Playa del Carmen

- **Price:** MXN $40.00 (for a single adult)
- **Duration:** 1 hour

From the ruins, take a *colectivo* on the side of the highway near the turnoff. If you end up in Tulum town, catch a *colectivo* on the highway near the ADO bus terminal.

Tip: *To catch a* colectivo *at night from the side of the highway, flash the little light on your cell phone repeatedly as the cars pass by.*

Goodbye Mexico

Now that you have visited the Mayan Riviera, start planning your next trip to Mexico. The entire country offers fantastic travel, but some of my favorite places (as well as the safest and least expensive) are also in the south, such as the states of Oaxaca and Chiapas.

Please take a look at *Your Chiapas Adventure: San Cristobal de las Casas and Palenque, Mexico*, my second guidebook published by Unanchor.

For all kinds of information on living and traveling in Mexico, please see my blog, *No Hay Bronca*.

Other Places to Go

This guide covers the five highlights of the region: Cancun, Valladolid, Chichén Itzá, Playa del Carmen, and Tulum. Of course, if you have more time, there's much more to see in the Mayan Riviera and Yucatán Peninsula, including reef-lined islands, broad beaches, remote ruins, pristine  *cenotes*, and dynamic cities full of culture—especially colonial Mérida west of Valladolid and colorful Campeche on the Gulf of Mexico.

Playa del Carmen is an excellent base for exploring surrounding destinations, so if you have a few extra days, I recommend staying there. But you could also choose a quieter base like Puerto Morelos or Akumal, which have fewer hotels and restaurants but not nearly as many people.

Tip: Don't make downtown Cancun your base for your entire trip. It's good for two or three nights—perhaps more but only if you have lots of time. It's not that downtown Cancun is bad, it's just that you can get better hotels for better prices in practically every other town on the Mayan Riviera, and they'll be walking distance from the beach.

Puerto Morelos

Puerto Morelos is a charming beachside town halfway between Cancun and Playa del Carmen, about 30 minutes by *colectivo* from both. If the *colectivo* drops you off on the side of the highway, look for another to take you into town 5-10 minutes away.

The sea is shallow and the reef is close, so confident swimmers can get to it with their flippers and snorkel gear. To the north is an undeveloped stretch of beach that's part of the Puerto Morelos Reef National Park.

Puerto Morelos has the usual fancy hotels and timeshares on the beach, and there are discount options in town by the road to the highway. It's great for either a day trip or to stay a few nights, with excellent fish restaurants and a tasteful artisanal market in the center of town.

On the highway about a mile south of the turn for Puerto Morelos is the Dr. Alfredo Barrera Marín Botanical Garden, which besides birds, iguanas, and spider monkeys also has a 4-km trail, suspension bridge, and Mayan ruins. It's open from 8 a.m. to 4 p.m. every day. The entrance is 120 pesos for foreigners, 100 for Mexicans, and 50 for Mexican students, teachers, and pensioners (with ID).

Inland from Puerto Morelos is the Boca del Puma adventure park and the Siete Bocas *cenote*.

In the other direction from Playa del Carmen is Akumal, a diving town on a secluded bay about halfway between Playa del Carmen and Tulum. Its tranquil beach and friendly village is a wonderful place to get some privacy and do a lot of scuba diving and snorkeling. The town is only .5 km from the highway, an easy walk from the *colectivo* drop-off.

You can learn about environmental issues at the Akumal Ecological Center and arrange scuba diving at the Akumal Dive Shop, both in town.

Just north of Akumal is the Yal-Ku Lagoon next to the sea, an fantastic spot for snorkeling with turtles and manta rays. Inland from Akumal is Aktun Chen Park with jungle trips, caving, and—of course—a *cenote*.

Between Playa del Carmen and Akumal is Puerto Aventuras, which like Playacar is a gated community that you can enter for free. Besides a nice beach, there's also an undeveloped section on the southern end with Mayan ruins and a crystal-clear inlet frequented by turtles and dolphins. Puerto Aventuras has restaurants, hotels, and a museum with artifacts from sunken ships.

Finally, you can find some nice places to stay in Tulum's hotel zone on the beach and plenty of discount hotels in Tulum town. Staying in Tulum is a good option if you plan on doing some exploring south of the Mayan Riviera, where there are more ruins, lots of jungle, and the enormous Sian Ka'an Biosphere Reserve.

For hotels in Puerto Morelos, Akumal, Puerto Aventuras, or Tulum, search Google Maps or booking.com, or in low-season just show up and have a look around.

Cozumel, Isla Mujeres, and Holbox Islands

Three gorgeous islands are easily reached from Cancun and Playa del Carmen: Cozumel, Isla Mujeres, and Holbox:

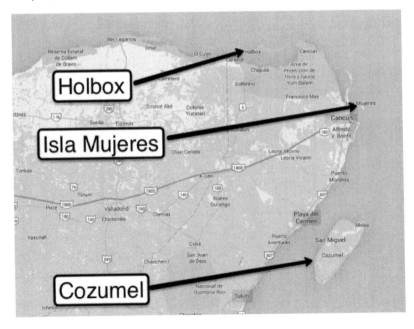

Cozumel

On a clear day you can see the hotels of Cozumel from Playa del Carmen. It's a big island covered with jungle and lined with beaches. Only 6% of Cozumel is developed, and it has an interesting history, too. Besides being an important Mayan population center, this was also where Cortés first landed in Mexico before traveling to Veracruz and then inland to the Valley of Mexico to conquer the Aztecs.

There are excellent dive sites all around the island, so good that Jaques Cousteau called it one of the most spectacular places for scuba diving in the world. But for info on diving, you can visit a Playa del Carmen dive shop first—they arrange dives there as well.

Cozumel is an easy day trip from Playa del Carmen—just walk to the ferry terminal, buy a ticket, and hop on. Several ferry companies make the trip all day, every day. The cheapest is Ultramar—at the time of writing a return ticket is 140 pesos.

The ferry disembarks in the town of San Miguel de Cozumel. Its pretty *zócalo* (center square) is a straight walk from the ferry dock. All around the *zócalo* are restaurants and shops, and there are a few banks with international ATMs if you need money.

As the ferry arrives, you'll see the big cruise ship docks to the south. Because of these cruise ships and the thousands of tourists who pour out of them daily, everything in Cozumel is overpriced, especially souvenirs. Because of this, to save money on lunch or a scooter rental, walk outside of the downtown core. Once you get off the pedestrian streets, things get a lot cheaper.

Some places to see in town include the small Cozumel Museum (Av. Rafael E. Melgar and Calle 4) and the Municipal Market (Calle Dr. Alfredo Rosado Salas between 20 and 25 Av), which has some inexpensive international restaurants. A good Mexican seafood restaurant is El Chino Marinero, which is one block from the market on Calle 1 and 20 Av.

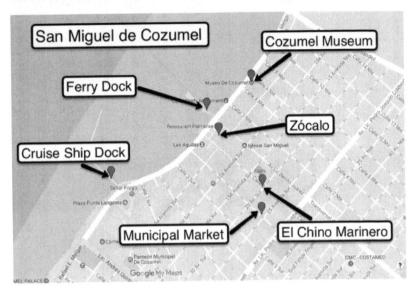

The coastline of San Miguel de Cozumel is a seawall next to the road. It's nice for a walk, but to go to a beach you'll need to hire a taxi or rent a car, 4-wheeler, or scooter. Again, you'll get better prices on all of these the farther you get from the ferry and cruise ship docks—three or four blocks away should suffice.

Most beaches are on the western shore, which faces Playa del Carmen, while the eastern shore is a rocky, wild coastline. A fun beach trip is to first go to Playa Palancar near the southern tip of the island. From there you can get a boat to El Cielo, a remote beach with crystal-clear, shallow water.

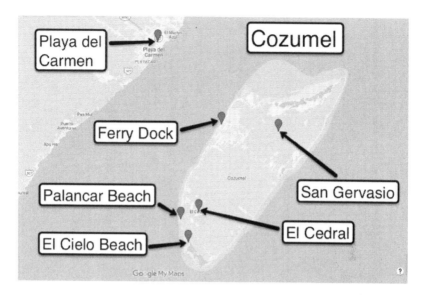

There are several Mayan sites on the island. Two of the biggest are San Gervasio and El Cedral. San Gervasio is up a bumpy dirt road, so if you want to take a rental car there, tell them at the rental office to confirm it's ok.

One more tip—when you go back to the ferry terminal to return to Playa del Carmen, make sure you get in the correct line. Several ferry companies leave from the same area and the lines can be very long.

Isla Mujeres has spacious beaches and a cool little village on the northern end of the island, with parks, ruins, and beach clubs farther south. It's a fun and easy day trip from Cancun or even Playa del Carmen, and there are lots of hotels if you want to spend the night. Like Cozumel, it has great snorkeling and dive sites, including the Underwater Museum of Art off the southern point, which has more than 400 life-sized sculptures.

Tip: Buy your goggles, snorkel, and flippers at Walmart—before your trip if you can. An inexpensive set may cost less than renting for a day or two.

Isla Mujeres

Though ferries to Isla Mujeres also leave from Cancun's Zona Hotelera (see **Day 1**), the cheaper ones leave from Puerto Juárez just north of downtown. From Tulum Av, catch a local bus going north with "Puerto Juárez" on the windshield. Ask the driver to let you off at the ferry terminals. If you don't speak Spanish, saying "Isla Mujeres" should suffice.

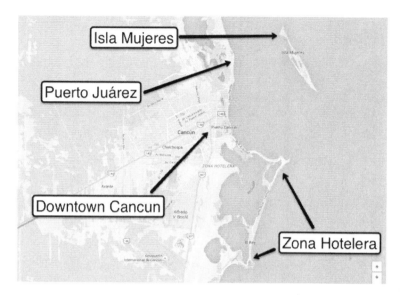

To save time, or if you have a group, a taxi from downtown Cancun straight to the ferry terminals should cost about 80 pesos.

There are two ferry companies in Puerto Juárez. Ultramar is more expensive and leaves more frequently, and Magaña is cheaper at 146 pesos for the return trip. Its final return, however, is earlier than Ultramar. At the time of writing, the last ship back is at 7:40 p.m. The terminals are within sight of each other, and you'll pass Ultramar first.

Once you get to Isla Mujeres, take a left out of the ferry terminal for the beaches, or walk straight ahead to visit the town. Across the water you can see Cancun's hotel skyline.

Isla Holbox

Holbox is too far away for a day trip, but if you have the time, you can stay on the island and visit some lovely beaches. Ferries leave from the town of Chiquila, but for now the ADO bus doesn't go there. Take the second-class Mayab bus, which leaves from the downtown Cancun ADO terminal. Ask at the terminal for the current schedule. The trip to Chiquila takes about three hours and the buses leave infrequently. Take a taxi if you want to save time, and as usual, negotiate the fare beforehand.

Beaches

Beach after beach line the coast, with many occupied by big resorts. Although Mexican law states that all waterfront is public land, if there's no public access point, you're out of luck. At some resorts you can buy a day pass for between $60 and $100 USD, which should include meals.

Hidden between the resorts, the public beaches on the Mayan Riviera are much less developed and more laid-back than Playa del Carmen and of course Cancun. Good ones include Tulum, Puerto Morelos, Akumal, Xpu-Ha, Xcacal, and Maroma. Look for them on a map and arrive by *colectivo* or taxi.

Xpu-Ha beach, one of the best, is about 20 minutes south of Playa del Carmen. To get there, take a *colectivo* from Playa toward Tulum, and tell the driver to let you off at Xpu-Ha (pronounced SHPOO-ha).

A little dirt road leads to the beach, and to use it you'll be charged 40 pesos. Once on the beach you can buy food and beer from the convenience store, rent chairs under the shade, have drinks and fresh seafood at an open-air bar, or simply stroll and swim down the tree-lined beach.

Remote Xcacel beach is a little farther south of Xpu-Ha. It's an important turtle nesting area that also has a campground.

North of Cancun, Isla Blanca is a long stretch of undeveloped beaches. It's a locals' favorite and a good kitesurfing spot. You'll have to rent a car to get there or negotiate for a taxi.

Ruins

Tulum and Chichén Itzá get all the attention, but ancient Mayan ruins have been discovered all over the Yucatán Peninsula, including El Rey on Cancun's Zona Hotelera (close to Playa Delfines) and nine on Cozumel (with San Gervasio as the standout).

After Tulum and Chichén Itzá, I'd say that Cobá is the next best nearby ruin complex. You can rent bicycles to explore the large site surrounded by jungle. The ruins are an hour inland from

Tulum town, and only one ADO bus from Tulum goes to Cobá and back every day. (Confirm on the ADO website.) Second-class buses are more frequent, but you'll have to go to the ADO bus terminal in Tulum town to ask for the schedule. Try to leave early and come back late—Cobá is big.

Other nearby sites include Muyil south of Tulum, El Meco by Puerto Juárez, and Ek Balam by Valladolid.

The biggest ancient Mayan city near the Mayan Riviera, however, is wild and barely-excavated Calakmul. To get there, you'll need to rent a car or speak decent Spanish to navigate public transportation.

Ruins both huge and tiny surround Mérida, and beyond are the massive ancient cities of Tikal in Guatemala to the south and Palenque in the Mexican state of Chiapas to the west.

Cenotes

The Mayan Riviera has more than 6,000 *cenotes*, with many set up for tourists around Valladolid and between Playa del Carmen and Tulum.

There's a cluster of four *cenote* parks across the street from the Barceló resort about 20 minutes south of Playa del Carmen (just before Xpu-Ha beach). Because of their proximity to Playa del Carmen and low entrance fees (100-200 pesos but bound to change), these four are convenient alternatives to Dos Ojos Cenote (recommended on **Day 5**), especially if you won't go to Tulum on the same day.

The first sign you'll see is for Kantun-Chi, which has five *cenotes* and an underground river. Cenote Cristiliano, Jardin del Eden Cenotes, and Cenote Azul come next, all within walking distance of each other, though Jardin del Eden is a little far from the highway. Like Dos Ojos, they're smaller-scale operations than the big adventure parks, so you just have to show up to get current prices and other information.

South of Xpu-Ha beach, the BioParque Lu'um Balam is another *cenote* option that also has caves and jungle walks.

Near Tulum, besides Gran Cenote you can also check out Zacil-ha and Aktun-ha. And between Valladolid and Chichén Itzá are the Dzitnup and Samula *cenotes* on the same property.

If you go to Mérida, then go to Cuzumá, which has the best *cenotes* I've ever seen. A narrow train track leads to three *cenotes* deep in the jungle. None have entrance fees—you just pay for the horse and little train.

Adventure Ecoparks

You can't miss the names: Xel-Ha, Xcaret, Xplor. From the moment you land at the Cancun airport, you'll see them everywhere, rivaling the nightclub Coco Bongo in ubiquitous promotion. They're also favorites of the guide/hustlers on Quinta Av in Playa del Carmen.

Note: Elsewhere in Mexico, the "x" is usually pronounced like an "h", as in México (ME-hee-co). But in the Mayan Riviera, it's usually pronounced like "sh", as in Xel-Ha (SHELL-ha), Xpu-Ha (SHPOO-ha), and many more. But there are exceptions—Xplor, for example, is pronounced how you'd expect (explore).

These places are big nature parks built around *cenotes* and beaches that have adventure activities and include all your food and drinks. If you want to go, I'm sure you'll have a good time, but remember that before you agree to a tour with someone you meet on the street, at least check the prices online to compare.

The ecoparks closest to Playa del Carmen are just south of Playacar: Xcaret, Xplor, and Rio Secreto. Xcaret is the largest and has Mayan ruins, dolphin shows, and an emphasis on culture. Xplor, owned by the same group as Xcaret, is more about adventure activities—it has an underground river and a big zipline tower that you can see from the highway.

Across the street is Rio Secreto, which is more than a *cenote*, but a tour through one mile of an underground river. Unlike smaller *cenotes* where you can just show up, for Rio Secreto you should make reservations on their website.

Near Tulum is Xel-Ha, another ecopark owned by Xcaret that they describe as an enormous natural aquarium. While these three major ecoparks that begin with "X" all have nature and water activities, perhaps you could say that Xplor is more about adrenaline, Xcaret is more about culture, and Xel-Ha is more family-oriented.

More on the Riviera

South of Cancun is Xochimilco Cancun, a reproduction of the famous canals and boat trips in Mexico City, and the Croco Cun interactive zoo, where you (and your kids) can explore the jungle on a guided tour and touch many of the native animals.

Between Puerto Morelos and Playa del Carmen are Rancho Bonanza, where you can ride horses in the jungle, and Cirque du Soliel, specializing in dinner shows.

Going south from Playa del Carmen, after Xcaret, you'll pass Punta Venado next, which is a small, isolated, pretty beach with a pleasant beach club. But the real draw—at least for me—is its mountain bike park, which has beginner trails but is definitely for people comfortable on a mountain bike. It's full of animals like iguanas, spider monkeys, coati, and crocodiles. Highly recommended.

And yes, there are even more places to visit between Cancun and Tulum! Practically the entire coast has been either developed or reserved in one way or another. These beaches, towns, and *cenotes* are all worth visiting in their own way, and just because some are much cheaper than others doesn't mean they aren't as nice.

Once again, you don't need a guide or tour for any of these places. Take a look at their websites and ask locals for tips and suggestions, such as the person at the front desk of your hotel. Be sure to check the locations on Google Maps—if it's close to the highway, then use a *colectivo*. If not, get ready to walk from the highway after the *colectivo* ride or take a taxi.

For places north of Playa del Carmen, take the *colectivo* to Cancun, and for places south, take the *colectivo* to Tulum. They both leave from Calle 2 between 15 and 20 Av in Playa del Carmen. Tell the driver your destination when you pay, and keep an eye open for signs in case he forgets.

Tip: To get back to Playa del Carmen or Cancun by colectivo, *walk out on the highway and wave at any passing white passenger van. They won't all stop—some are private charters—but it shouldn't take long for one with empty space to pick you up. After dark, flash the light on your cell phone.*

Mérida

If you loved Valladolid and want more *yucateca* culture, then go to Mérida, the capital of Yucatán state. Mérida is one of Mexico's most interesting, attractive, and culturally important cities, with colonial architecture, great museums, and a massive market packed with jungle fruit, huge *chaya* (a Yucatán herb) juices, and spicy *cochinita pibil* tacos.

Like Valladolid, Mérida's cathedral is built from the stones of plundered Mayan ruins:

In Mérida there are lots of hotels around the *zócalo* and cheapies by the bus terminal. Buses go to Mérida from everywhere, but the straightest shot is from Cancun. From Valladolid, Mérida is about two hours away.

And beyond...

Because of its location and the abundance of cheap flights to the international airport, Cancun is a logical starting point for longer trips in Mexico or Central America. If you are headed west into Mexico, then pass through Mérida and Campeche and points in between, or take an overnight trip straight to Palenque, a good travel hub. If you are headed south, then cross into Belize at Chetumal.

Please see my blog No Hay Bronca for travel information about Mexico and Central America.

Thanks a lot and come back soon! ¡*Hasta pronto!*

Things You Need to Know

Cancun and the Mayan Riviera

Cancun is on the northeast corner of the Yucatán Peninsula in Mexico. The three places you stay in this itinerary—Cancun, Valladolid, and Playa del Carmen—form a rough triangle:

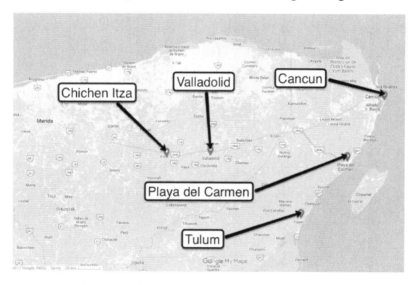

You can visit these places in any order you like. If you decide to stay at a resort in Cancun or Playa del Carmen, then you can visit Valladolid, Chichén Itzá, and Tulum on long day trips.

Let me tell you a secret—you can skip Cancun. If you are on a budget and want to walk barefoot from your hotel to the beach every day, then go straight to Playa del Carmen. It may not be world-famous like Cancun, but it isn't fully in the shadow of huge resorts and mass tourism either. ADO, the bus from the airport to downtown Cancun, also has a direct bus to Playa del Carmen.

But do you really want to fly all the way to Mexico and not see Cancun? With good connections and a fast check-in at your hotel, you can get from the airport to the beach in about an hour.

Places on the coast (Cancun, Playa del Carmen, Tulum) are in the state of Quintana Roo, which is in the eastern time zone, like New York City. On the other hand, most places inland are in the state of Yucatán (Valladolid, Chichén Itzá, Mérida), which is in the central time zone, like Mexico City and Chicago. So plan accordingly when you travel between them.

A Brief History

The known history of the Yucatán begins with the Mayans, a civilization that peaked during its Classic period (c. AD 250 to 900). During this time, great cities like Chichén Itzá were constructed. Mayan cities were governed as city-states and regular wars broke out between them.

Though the civilization collapsed around 1250 (scientists still cannot agree upon why), the Mayan people still exist, especially in southern Mexico and Guatemala, making up the largest indigenous population of the Americas. Mayans have many cultural subdivisions with separate languages and traditions. The Maya of the Yucatán are one of the largest of such groups.

By the time the Spanish arrived in 1517, great cities like Chichén Itzá, Tikal, and Palenque were already abandoned and lost in the jungle. It is believed that the name Yucatán came about as a misunderstanding between the Spanish and natives. The Spanish asked, "Where are we?" and the natives replied "I don't understand," which the Spanish heard as "Yucatán" and assumed was the name of the region.

The conquest of the Yucatán by Francisco de Montejo (el Adelantado), who made his capital in Mérida, occurred in 1537, a decade after the conquest of central Mexico by Cortes. Valladolid was founded on May 28, 1543 by Montejo's nephew Francisco de Montejo (el Sobrino) after the conquest of the easternYucatán.

The Yucatán's incorporation into independent Mexico came in stages, and at various times the Yucatán was a separate nation. Bad treatment of the Mayans by the Spanish-descended population led to several wars and revolutions, including the Canek rebellion (1761) and the Caste War (1847-1901).

Now, the Yucatán is the safest part of Mexico. The development of mass tourism, starting with Cancun in the 1970s, has provided steady employment and tourist dollars.

When to Go

In Mexico, many places operated by the government, like museums and tourist information booths, are closed on Monday. This does not include major ruins like Chichén Itzá and Tulum.

Mexico has three high seasons: *Semana Santa*, which is the week before Easter Sunday; December to mid-January, especially between Christmas and New Year's; and July to August. Expect higher prices and more tourists during high season. If you are on a budget, don't even think about traveling here during super-high season: *Semana Santa* and around Christmas.

The check-in and check-out lines at big resorts and hotels can get quite long on busy travel days, such as Mexican holidays and most weekends. If possible, try not to check in on Friday or Saturday afternoon and check out on Sunday morning.

Much is made of the spring and fall equinoxes at Chichén Itzá. Shadows moving on the Castillo pyramid resemble a slithering snake. Except huge crowds at the ruins and full hotels in Valladolid.

Mexico has festivals year round. A quick Google search will tell you what's happening when you want to go. Two of the biggest music festivals in Playa del Carmen are the BPM Festival (electronic music) in January and the Riviera Maya Jazz Festival in late November.

Transportation

In this itinerary, you use buses and *colectivos* (passenger vans). In general, buses are better for longer distances (Cancun to Valladolid, Valladolid to Playa del Carmen) and *colectivos* are better for shorter distances (Cancun to Playa del Carmen, Playa del Carmen to Tulum, Valladolid to Chichén Itzá). Prices in this guide are subject to change.

Leaving Playa del Carmen

If your flight leaves in the late afternoon or at night, check out of your hotel (usually before noon) and leave your bags behind the front desk while you explore Tulum or elsewhere.

Once you get back to Playa del Carmen, take one more swim, eat one more meal, and buy some souvenirs. Quinta Av has everything, but if you want tequila, buy it at a supermarket or corner store for cheaper than at the airport duty free shop. Wrap the bottle(s) in your clothes in your checked luggage. Find out how many you can bring home—for example, recently the maximum you can bring into the U.S. was raised to three liters.

Bus to Cancun Airport

- **Price:** MXN $178.00 (for a single adult)
- **Duration:** 1 hour

Buses to the Cancun airport leave from both ADO bus terminals in Playa del Carmen. Remember that for international flights you should arrive three hours early, especially because the airport is relatively small but can get very busy.

It's a good idea to buy bus tickets a few days in advance. If your hotel is closer to the second bus station, buy them there, as the bus from the main station stops there on the way to the airport.

The bus takes about one hour and 20 minutes and leaves every hour or half hour. You can check the schedule at the ADO website.

The Cancun airport has three terminals. Be sure to get off at the right one according to the airline you're flying with. Listen for the driver's announcement in Spanish or check the airline directory beforehand.

The Cancun Airport

It's modern, clean, and safe, and most people speak English. You can take the ADO bus between the airport and downtown Cancun or Playa del Carmen or consider numerous taxi options.

The most important thing to know about the airport is which of the three terminals you will depart from. They are determined by airline, and you can check a directory here[1].

A free shuttle travels between terminals. It's really slow, and you should ignore the pickup time displayed at the stop. It takes less than 10 minutes to walk between Terminals 2 and 3. Terminal 1 is far from the other two, but it's really only used by Aeromexico.

---

1 http://www.cancun-airport.com/airlines-directory.htm

Important: Tequila is cheaper at a grocery store than at the airport duty free shop, and of course souvenirs are much cheaper anywhere else.

If you plan on visiting other parts of Mexico, look into domestic flights before you commit to a long-distance bus ride. Mexico's domestic airlines have discounted fares, often cheaper than the first-class bus.

Buses

ADO is the first-class bus company. Check their website at https://www.ado.com.mx/ for schedules and prices. At the time of writing it's only in Spanish, but easy to use.

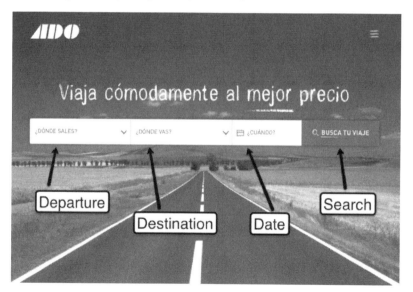

If you're not sure which date you'll be traveling, just guess. The schedules are the same (or nearly the same) every day.

Note: *If you search for buses more than a month in advance, you might not see all the options. So just search for any date within a week or two to get an idea of the schedule, and then search the actual date later, when you are ready to buy tickets.*

If you see a little arrow next to the place name, it means that it has more than one bus station. For Playa del Carmen, for example, the choices are:

- Playa del Carmen Alterna, Q. Roo.
- Playa del Carmen, Q. Roo.

In this case, "Alterna" is the second bus station, which is away from the beach. So choose the regular one, unless of course your hotel is closer to the second bus station.

The Cancun airport is listed as "Aeropuerto Cancun, Q. Roo." Once you start typing "Cancun" it should come up as a suggestion.

Here's the next page you see. This example is for the Cancun airport to downtown Cancun.

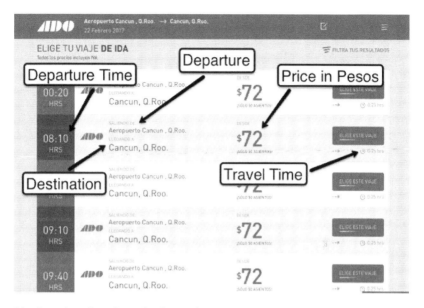

Notice that for the trip from the airport to downtown, all the prices and travel times are the same.

Below is the schedule for downtown Cancun to Valladolid. Notice that the cheaper fares have a little tag with a percentage symbol next to them. That's because if you buy the tickets in advance online, you can get a discount. (Not recommended for the airport bus in case your plane arrives late.)

If you understand Spanish and don't mind taking the time to set up an account, you can buy and print tickets beforehand. But don't do this unless you're sure your plans won't change—although the triple-digit discounts look big in pesos, it might not actually be so much in your own currency.

Also, due to the convenient locations of bus terminals and the fact that buses depart frequently, instead of constraining yourself to a schedule by pre-purchasing tickets, you can usually just show up and buy them before your trip.

If you travel during busy season, however, or will use a route with only one bus per day, like between Chichén Itzá and Playa del Carmen, then getting advance tickets may be a good idea. But remember that you can also buy them in advance from a bus terminal.

When you ask for tickets at the bus terminal, they assume that you want the first-class ADO buses. To save money, ask for a second-class bus.

- *¿Hay un autobús de segunda clase?*
  Is there a second-class bus?

There's nothing wrong with the second-class buses, except they may take a little longer by making more stops or taking indirect routes. So be sure to compare the travel time with the first-class bus.

Tip: *Always choose the seats closest to the front of the bus. You'll be the first one on and off, and you'll be far from the bathroom. Also, always bring a sweater on longer bus rides—they tend to crank the air conditioning. Earplugs can be useful too because of overly loud movies in Spanish.*

Colectivos

Colectivos, also known as *combis*, run between Cancun and Playa del Carmen, Valladolid and Chichén Itzá, and Playa del Carmen and Tulum. They're cheaper and faster than the bus. In Playa del Carmen, the *colectivos* going north to Cancun and south to Tulum (and all points in between) leave four blocks from the ADO bus terminal:

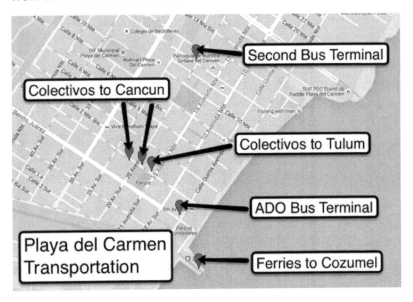

In downtown Cancun, *colectivos* for Playa del Carmen leave from the parking lot outside the ADO bus terminal and also from a parking lot next to Comercial Mexicana across Tulum Av.

Catch local buses on Tulum Av to the Zona Hotelera (the beach) or Puerto Juárez (the departure point for Isla Mujeres). Their destinations are written on the windshields, and be sure to wait on the correct side of the street.

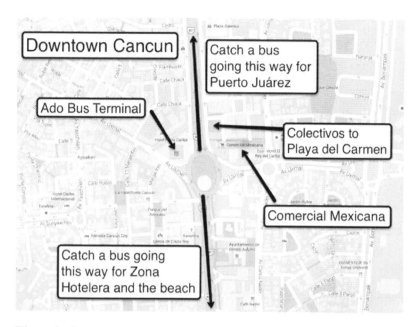

Though the drivers may not speak English, *colectivos* are typically hassle-free. If you don't speak Spanish and are going somewhere less common than Tulum or Playa del Carmen, write it on a piece of paper and keep an eye open for signs for your destination in case the driver forgets about you. Smile at other passengers, who should be happy to help. Unless they ask beforehand, usually you pay when you get out. Bring a pocketful of change if you can, especially for a day with multiple trips. Don't pay with a 500-peso bill, nor a 200 unless the total of your group's fares is more than 100 pesos.

Taxis

Taxis are easy to find if you need one. They don't have meters, so agree on a price before you get in. If you don't speak Spanish, have a piece of paper and a pencil ready to write numbers on.

If you want a taxi for a longer ride, ask your hotel to call a service for you. This way you'll know that the taxi is safe and you can avoid getting overcharged, as the person at the front desk will get the price for you.

Renting a Car

The transportation instructions in this guide assume that you will use buses and *colectivos*. But you may consider renting a car, especially if you travel in a large group. With the low prices of car rentals, you might find that the total cost of the rental car, gas, and parking is comparable or even cheaper than the total of bus tickets for everyone in your group.

Plus, you will save time getting to places like Valladolid and Chichén Itzá, where the bus may make stops on the way. In fact, if you want to see Chichén Itzá on a day trip, renting a car is the way to go—it's just too far from Cancun to take the bus there and back and still have time to see everything.

In addition, with a rental car you can go to less-visited, inland places like the Mayan ruins of Cobá without planning your day around the bus schedule.

But if you're alone or with only one other person and will mostly stay on the coast between Cancun and Tulum, then you'll get around just fine by *colectivo*. Also, while traffic isn't much of a problem on the Mayan Riviera, one-lane streets in party towns like Playa del Carmen can get congested on a Friday or Saturday night.

So, besides the number of people in your group and the places you want to visit, when deciding whether or not to rent a car also think about parking. Many of the smaller hotels recommended in this guide do not have parking lots. If you park on the street, be sure that no valuables are visible in your car.

All the usual international rental companies are available in the Mayan Riviera. These companies have offices at the Cancun airport: Enterprise, Europcar, Budget, Dollar, Alamo, National, Ace, Advantage, Payless, Fox, Firefly, and more.

You can get big discounts through a third-party website like expedia.com, but be aware that the insurance they offer is not valid in Mexico. When you get to the counter to pick up your car, the price will double or even triple once they add insurance. So also look directly on the car rental company website and read all the fine print.

If you only want the car for part of your trip, pick it up at the airport and then drop it off at a car rental office somewhere else (Cancun, Playa del Carmen, etc.), or vice versa.

Hertz, Budget, Thrifty, Europcar, Avis, and Sixt have offices within walking distance from the beach in Playa del Carmen. In Cancun, most offices (including Hertz, Alamo, National, Budget, and Europcar) are a 15- to 30-minute walk (or 5-minute taxi ride) from the ADO terminal. An exception is the Europcar office about 10 minutes walking to the southwest from Parque las Palapas, and the Hertz office in the hotel zone.

Or, once in Mexico, you could visit a travel agency or an independent car rental office to get a quote. There are many in Playa del Carmen on Calles 6 and 8 between Quinta and 10 Av., or in Cancun on and around Tulum Av.

Driving in Mexico can be somewhat challenging, although the well-traveled roads in the Mayan Riviera are mostly flat, straight, and pothole-free. Also, the drivers seem more laid-back than in other parts of Mexico, like Mexico City, where aggression is the order of the day.

If you drink, don't drive—besides the obvious reasons, police checkpoints are often set up on the highway between Cancun and Tulum, and there are a few permanent ones too. Slow down to drive through them, but don't stop unless the police clearly signal you to do so.

Hotels

Many visitors to the Mayan Riviera stay in a resort. These all-inclusive monstrosities can be a good deal. You'll be right on the beach, have a pool, get unlimited food and drinks, and all-in-all have a fun, relaxing vacation.

The downside is that getting out into real-life Mexico is unlikely. Why would you venture into downtown Cancun for *salbutes* when you have a free buffet in your luxury hotel? Why would you travel inland to Valladolid when the pool party starts at 10 a.m. every day?

The hotels recommended in this itinerary are smaller, more modest, and much cheaper. If you are comfortable doing so, then it's easy to arrive with no reservations and spend a little time walking around looking at hotels (not during super-high season, though—see **When to Go**).

Many hotels have prices posted behind the front desk. Always ask to see the room before you take it. Peek into the bathroom. Try the shower and air conditioner or fan.

Some people stay in dorm beds in hostels. In Cancun they're your cheapest option, but in Playa del Carmen they may be the same price as a single room in a small hotel. Stay in a hostel if you want to meet people, not if you want to get some rest.

Please remember that hotel prices change, especially with the peso's ongoing loss of value against the U.S. dollar. In my travels I've seen backpackers quoting prices from guidebooks when haggling for a room—please don't do that! But do tell them that their hotel was recommended in this one.

One more thing—if you decide to follow this itinerary and get hotels on the fly, pack light! For tips on packing for a trip to Mexico, please see this article[2].

Reservations

If getting off the bus in a new town in a new country, wandering around looking at hotels, and trying to communicate in Spanish doesn't appeal to you, then make reservations beforehand. Many of the hotels in this itinerary have a website.

Or search Google Maps, booking.com, or whichever travel website you like. Check the location of the hotel to be sure it's within walking distance of the bus terminal.

Resorts

Big discounts abound for all-inclusive vacations to the Mayan Riviera. Go to a travel agent or take a look at websites like booking.com. If you know Spanish, check out despegar.com, Mexico's travel booking website.

---

[2] https://nohaybronca.wordpress.com/2015/12/03/what-to-pack-for-a-trip-to-mexico/

Besides Cancun's hotel zone, the entire coast has huge resort compounds with private beaches, multiple all-you-can-eat restaurants, and free drinks all day long. These are great places to get away from it all, and in fact many people never leave them during their trip. While resorts do offer overpriced tours to ruins and *cenotes*, remember that going on your own isn't only cheaper, but more adventurous.

The beach in Playa del Carmen is lined with nice four- and five-story hotels, some all-inclusive. Many have private pools, bars, and restaurants. You might be able to find a deal before you go, or you could easily walk down Quinta Av and ask at the front desk of any place that catches your fancy.

Airbnb

Airbnb has quickly become an excellent alternative to hotels, especially in Playa del Carmen. With Airbnb you rent someone's room, apartment, or entire house. It's great for saving money on longer-term stays, and you might find a stylish place with a kitchen, swimming pool, patio, and rooftop access.

Airbnb.com is easy to use and you don't need an account to look at what's available—just type in your destination and the dates.

Restaurants

As a sweeping generalization, you'll encounter three kinds of restaurants on this trip:

1. Foreign restaurants

In Cancun and Playa del Carmen you'll see burgers, pizza, Italian food, sushi—you name it. It may be good but will definitely be more expensive than real Mexican food.

If you want something fancy, go to the Zona Hotelerain Cancun orlook around Quinta Av in Playa del Carmen.

2. Mexican restaurants geared towards foreign tourists

Beware the Mexican food in these places. Mexicans tend to think that foreigners don't like spicy food, so they dumb it down. If a tired basket of nachos sits on every table and the salsa tastes like marinara sauce, then you're in the wrong place.

It's good to ask locals for advice, like at the front desk of your hotel, but explain that you want something real. Otherwise you'll be directed to a restaurant with the "Americanized" Mexican food they think foreigners like. The truth is, most people do like this stuff. It's like the Mexican food you get back home, but better. But it doesn't come close to the real thing—what you eat in Valladolid's Bazar Municipal.

Speaking of nachos—like burritos, they are an American invention,whether by an American or a *chicano* (Mexican

American), who knows. So unless you are at Señor Frogs or another tequila-shooter franchise restaurant, don't order nachos. You will get 7-11-style pump-cheese garbage.

3. Real Mexican restaurants, geared toward Mexican tourists or locals

Learn how to spot these places. You can get some real tacos if you see this:

The recommendations in this itinerary are restaurants that serve real Mexican food, especially regional food. Experiment and be courageous. If it's true that you can't handle the spice, tell them. You'll get the same food, minus the salsa, which is much better than pump-cheese nachos.

Quick Language Tip:
- *¿Es picante?*
  Is it spicy?

- *Menos picante por favor*
  Less spicy please

Food and Drinks

This is not an exhaustive list, just some tasty suggestions to get you started:

Regional Yucatán Food

Cochinita pibil: Shredded pork marinated in spicy red *achiote* sauce. You can get it in tacos, *tortas* (Mexican sandwich), *panuchos,* or *salbutes. Achiote* can also be used to cook fish, shrimp, or something else that's surely delicious.

Relleno negro: Turkey cooked in a black paste, served as stew or in tacos.

Sopa de lima: Turkey, lime, and tortilla soup. It may not sound like much, but many claim that it's the best meal in the Yucatán.

Lomitos de Valladolid: As the name suggests, a specialty from Valladolid, featuring chunks of pork (not shredded like *cochinita pibil*) with a special tomato, chili, and garlic sauce.

Poc chuc: More pork! This time grilled and with an orange marinade.

Pepián: A Guatemalan chicken stew that you can also find in Mexico. The vegetables and seasoning included depend on the chef putting it together.

Panuchos: Meat, often *cochinita pibil*, on a flat, black bean-covered tortilla.

Salubutes: Meat, often *cochinita pibil*, on a puffy tortilla.

Polcanes: Something like a crispy *salubutes* shell stuffed with ground pumpkin seeds, if that makes any sense. It should be vegetarian but confirm this—in Mexico, you never know.

Tip: *When you go to a casual regional restaurant for the first time, like Antojitos Sandra in Playa del Carmen or the food stands in Parque las Palapas in downtown Cancun, order one (or three) of everything: one sopa, one panucho, one empanada, etc. Try them all and then go back for more once you know what you like best.*

Mexican Food

Tacos: Real tacos are a palm-sized corn tortilla with meat (try *pastor*, marinated pork from a huge vertical spit), salsa, lime, cilantro, and onion. You can get them with *queso* (cheese). They often come in orders of five.

Tacos dorados: Fried tacos; a long rolled-up tortilla covered in lettuce, cream, and cheese. Also called *flautas* (flutes).

Enchiladas: Similar to *tacos dorados* but not fried. Rolled-up tortillas filled with chicken and drenched with green or red sauce.

Quesadillas: A tortilla folded in half with cheese and a wide variety of meat or vegetable fillings.

Gringas: Meat, usually *pastor*, inside a flour tortilla with cheese, like a *quesadilla*.

Sopes: Like a *tostada* (meat, lettuce, onion, and cheese on a hard tortilla), but over a thick, soft tortilla.

Empanadas: Something stuffed into a pastry-like shell—meat, cheese, corn and cheese, or seafood.

Huaraches: A long flat oval tortilla with meat, beans, cheese, salsa, and lettuce.

Tortas: Mexican sandwiches with choice of meat, cheese, and some vegetables.

Pozole: Red soup with chicken, corn, lettuce, onion, avocado, and more.

Seafood

Seafood comes in all the ways you'd expect, including in soups, tacos, tostadas, and empanadas. Octopus (*pulpo*)is especially good in Mexico because they beat it with a flat piece of metal before cooking it, so it's not too chewy. Shrimp (*camarones*)come in many ways, even covered in melted cheese and bacon. And though pricy, lobster (*langosta*) is delicious as usual, but remember that warm-water lobsters don't have claws.

You can ask for a menu in English, or try these Mexican-style favorites:

Pescado: Fish, typically the whole thing served with a small salad, rice, French fries, or nachos. Bring your Spanish dictionary to decipher all the choices, such as *frito* (fried), *empanizado* (breaded), *al mojo de ajo* (with garlic), or *a la diabla* (spicy). If you don't want the entire fish, order a *filete* (fillet).

Cóctel: A seafood cocktail with red sauce, onions, avocado, cilantro, and tomatoes. Eat them with crackers or nachos, and beer, of course. Order *camarones* (shrimp), *pulpo* (octopus), *ostiones* (oysters), or *pescado*.

Empanadas: Small pocket-pies (for the lack of a better description). Seafood ones come with *camarones*, *pulpo*, *ostiones*, or *pescado*. They're great to carry down to the beach.

Fruit

Mexico is fruit heaven. Look for *cócteles de fruta*, fruit cocktails, served in small restaurants or on the street, such as between the church and the Cozumel dock in Playa del Carmen.

Or buy fruit from a market or *frutería* (fruit store). The pink fruit in the photo below is *pitahaya* (dragon fruit):

Fresh Fruit Juice

A great way to get your fruit is to drink it in a *jugo* (juice), *licuado* (more like a shake or smoothie), or *agua* (a watered-down juice, always served with set lunches). Many restaurants sell these, but they are cheapest from a juice stand, which are often found in markets. A liter of freshly-squeezed orange or grapefruit juice should cost 30 or 40 pesos.

Chaya is an herb from the state of Yucatán commonly used in infusions or mixed with orange or pineapple juice. Look for it—very refreshing on a hot day.

Water

Yes, it's true that you shouldn't drink tap water in Mexico unless you stay in a nice hotel where they explicitly tell you it's ok. The glasses left in your bathroom are for mixing drinks, not drinking the water. Some hotels do provide drinking water—ask at the front desk—but if not, you'll have to buy it.

If you're staying in one place for more than four or five days, you can save money by buying a *garrafón*, the big 20-liter bottle of water. Keep it in your hotel room and use it to fill smaller bottles when you go out for the day.

Note: *These bottles are large and heavy. You can also find 10- and 5-liter bottles, which at 20 or 25 pesos are also a much better value than the smaller bottles of water that sell for 10 or 15 pesos.*

Look for *garrafónes* stacked up in small convenience stores. They cost about 30 pesos, and there's a deposit for the bottle of about 50. Make sure you get a receipt so you can return the bottle. Some places, including the ubiquitous convenience store OXXO, may not accept bottle returns, so in that case look for a smaller, more local store. If you don't speak Spanish, try saying:

- *Quiero comprar un garrafón, y ¿Puedo devolver la botella luego?*
  I'd like to buy a garrafón, and can I return the bottle later?
- *¿Me puedes dar el ticket?*
  Can you give me a receipt?

(Yes, the English word *ticket* means *receipt* in Spanish, though you could also use *recibo*.)

Of course you could probably find a clerk who speaks English. If not, keep trying and you'll get your point across.

When you ask for water in a restaurant, you will get bottled water, which you'll have to pay for. Therefore glasses of water don't come automatically to everyone at the table like they do in other countries. And please don't obsess over ice. It's pointless to ask the waitress if the ice is safe—do you think she would actually say no? Remember, if bars and restaurants used dirty ice for their drinks, everyone would get sick—locals too— and put them out of business.

Beer and Tequila

Corona is everywhere, but try Bohemia or the regional Superior for a better lager. If you prefer dark beer try Victoria, Indio, or Negra Modelo. To save money, buy a *caguama* (40 oz.) at an OXXO convenience store. You pay a deposit for the bottle, so save the receipt.

Craft beer is slowly developing in Mexico. It'll be expensive on a restaurant menu, or you can try Tulum beer, now sold at 7-11. (It's ok.)

Yes, there are oh-so many delicious tequilas in Mexico! Remember that if you buy tequila in a souvenir shop it will be wildly overpriced. Go to a supermarket, like Comercial Mexicana. For higher-end, affordable tequila, I like 1800, Patrón, and Milagro.

Money Matters

ATMs, Credit Cards & the Currency

Mexico's currency is the peso. Check exchange rates before arriving in country.

Forget traveler's checks—you get the best exchange rate by withdrawing from an ATM. Use ATMs at banks, not the ones in OXXO convenience stores or restaurants, which have higher fees.

In Cancun, look for banks on Tulum Av south of the ADO bus terminal. In Playa del Carmen, several banks (Banamex, Santander, and Bancomer) are on Benito Juárez near 25 Av. There's also a Bannorte on 10 Av between Calle 8 and Calle 10, and a Scotiabank on 10 Av and Constituyentes.

In Valladolid, two banks (Bancomer and Banamex) are on the *zócalo*, and there's an international HSBC ATM in the Bazar Municipal.

To save the most you can on fees, match the sticker on the ATM with the symbol on the back of your card, such as Cirrus, Plus, The Exchange, or Interac:

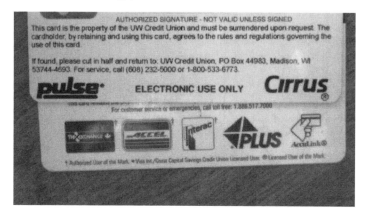

I recommend using cash at restaurants and stores. If you use a credit card, keep a record and check your statement when you get home. If the wrong person gets ahold of your credit card number, they can run up lots of charges. Banks will usually reimburse your money if this happens.

When eating at restaurants, check the bill carefully. Foreigners—mainly those who don't speak Spanish—are sometimes overcharged, especially when drinking.

Many restaurants, souvenir shops, and travel agencies will accept U.S. dollars, but always pay in pesos because the exchange rate they use to convert to dollars will be outrageous. Exceptions are places where the price is always in dollars—usually only the big ecoparks (Xel-ha, etc.) or nightclubs (Coco Bongo, etc.).

Haggling + Tipping

If you don't see a posted price, expect to haggle. It's the norm in markets and some shops, and in many cases it's necessary to get a reasonable price. Don't be afraid to ask for a huge discount—like offering half of what you were quoted. Stay calm and pleasant. Don't get excited, angry, or impatient. Seem very non-committal. The best way to seek out a good price is to ask at several stores in view of each other and compare. Or make a deal: "How much for five shirts then?"

Remember, good-natured haggling doesn't oblige you to buy anything. If you don't want to buy, simply thank the vendor and walk away.

That said, there's no reason to drive a hard bargain when you're buying a bag of fruit at a non-touristy market, like in Valladolid. Although they may raise the price a little because you are a rich foreigner (can you blame them?), it shouldn't be unreasonable. The less you seem like a clueless tourist, the better. Take some time. Ask about the different fruit, what it's called. Accept any free samples.

In restaurants and bars, tip 10% on food and drinks. Check your bill carefully to be sure it wasn't already included. At the hotel, if a guy shows you to your room, tip him 10-20 pesos, more if he carries your bags. If you don't want to tip this guy, then thank him in the lobby and tell him you'll find the room by yourself.

Mexicans don't tip taxi drivers, although the ones in the Mayan Riviera seem to expect it because of so many foreign tourists. For a short trip, an extra 10 or 20 pesos won't break your budget, and for a longer trip or an extra friendly driver, drop a 50 or 100.

Also, give a peso or two to the grocery bagger at a big supermarket like Comercial Mexicana or Walmart.

For more about managing your money in Latin America (and the world), please see my article here[3].

Safety

At the time of writing, Mexico's crime and drug war problems as reported in the media don't apply to tourists in the Yucatán.

---

[3] http://www.transitionsabroad.com/listings/travel/articles/how-to-safely-manage-money-latin-america.shtml

As long as you stick to tourist areas (everything on this itinerary) and take some basic precautions, you'll be fine. Don't look at your map in public when lost. Don't wander down dark streets at night. Don't accept drinks from strangers.

Don't carry your camera around your neck; put it in your bag. Put your wallet in your front pocket. Don't leave your purse hanging from a restaurant chair. And—the most important rule—if someone gives you a bad vibe, firmly say goodbye and walk away.Many travelers all over the world have gotten into bad situations simply because they didn't want to be rude to a rude person.

If you're concerned, talk to the locals—the person at the front desk of your hotel, for example—to find out where not to go and what not to do.

Regardinghygiene, yes it's true that you can't drink the water in Mexico. (This is true in most parts of the world.) But don't worry—around here 99% of restaurants, bars and clubs use bottled water for drinks and ice.

The best way to prevent a food-borne illness is to never eat in an empty restaurant. If it's empty, it's empty for a reason. But remember that Mexicans eat lunch later, usually between 2 and 4 p.m., so plenty of good restaurants might be empty at noon or 5 p.m.

If you get sick, go to a pharmacy. You'll see them everywhere in Cancun and Playa del Carmen, and there are a few in central Valladolid. Get some medicine, and if it's serious, in many pharmacies you can talk to a doctor, often for free, who will prescribe antibiotics to clear it up right away. If you don't take medicine, food poisoning can last weeks.

For more on safety in Mexico, please read this[4].

Useful Spanish Phrases

I have included a few Spanish phrases in the itinerary. Try to listen to how they are pronounced—although English and Spanish have many similar words (called cognates), the pronunciation can be quite different.

If you don't speak any Spanish, I recommend spending a couple weeks before your trip learning the basics. Though many people in the Mayan Riviera speak English, try not to expect them to. Even if they do speak English, beginning with Spanish shows respect. Also, it will give you satisfaction to communicate with locals in their native language.

To be polite, Mexicans use a specific greeting before engaging in any communication, such as in a store, restaurant, or hotel. Use these at the right time of day:

- *Buenos días*
  Good morning
- *Buenas tardes*
  Good afternoon
- *Buenas noches*
  Good night (in the sense of *hello*, not *goodbye*)

After using the correct greeting, the beginning Spanish speaker should start every exchange with:

- *¿Habla usted inglés? No hablo español.*
  Do you speak English? I don't speak Spanish

---

4   https://nohaybronca.wordpress.com/2014/12/02/now-really-is-mexico-safe-or-not/

If the answer is yes, then no problem—switch to English. If the answer is no, then pull out your Spanish notes and use body language to communicate. A pencil and piece of paper is handy when haggling, buying bus tickets, or getting a taxi.

Other useful words:

- *Hola*
  Hello
- *Adiós*
  Goodbye
- *Sí, no*
  Yes, no
- *Por favor*
  Please
- *Gracias*
  Thank you. Also *no thank you* (When someone wants to sell you something that you don't want, a quick *gracias* with a firm tone of voice conveys *no thanks*. If you apologize or feign interest, they will persist and may become a nuisance).
- *Disculpe*
  Sorry/excuse me—used to get someone's attention (or apologize)
- *Con Permiso*
  Excuse me—used when you want someone to let you pass by
- *¿Mande?*
  The Mexican way to ask *What?* when you don't understand
- *Perdón, no entiendo*
  Sorry, I don't understand

If you can remember those, you're on your way. Don't buy a phrasebook—you can find all the basics online. Write them down and practice to memorize them. You can continue learning Mexican Spanish for travelers with my suggestions in this article[5].

Or, if you really want to learn Spanish, get a book. Sitting on a bus or beach is a great opportunity to do some studying.

Places and Terminology

Autobús / Camión: Words for *bus* in Mexican Spanish.

Centro, i.e. Centro Cancún: Downtown, in this case downtown Cancun.

Cenote: A freshwater limestone sinkhole leading to caves. Pronounced *se-NO-te.* They are everywhere in the Yucatán Peninsula and many are developed for tourism. There are two in Chichén Itzá, though you can't swim in them.

Cenote Zací: A *cenote* in Valladolid. You can swim in it, but being in a town it isn't crystal-clear like other *cenotes*.

Cenote Dos Ojos: One of many *cenote* parks between Playa del Carmen and Tulum. It has clear water and is great for swimming and scuba diving. Scuba and snorkel gear can be rented there.

Colectivo: A passenger van for short-term travel, which is often faster, cheaper, and more frequent than the bus. Notable *colectivos* go between Cancun and Playa del Carmen, Valladolid and Chichén Itzá, and Playa del Carmen and Tulum.

Cozumel: An island off Playa del Carmen.

---

5 https://nohaybronca.wordpress.com/2014/03/01/a-spanish-cheat-sheet-for-travelers-in-mexico/

D.F.: Distrito Federal, how you say *Mexico City* in Spanish, like how people say D.C. for Washington. Pronounced *de-EFF-eh*.

Isla Mujeres: An island off Cancun. Translates as "Ladies' Island," supposedly named for goddess images found there in the 16th century.

Kukulkán: An important Mayan king/god. The Castillo pyramid at Chichén Itzá, aka the Kukulkán pyramid, was his temple. Also, it's the name of the road that follows the beach in Cancún's Zona Hotelera.

Mercado: Market. Cancun's are touristy but good for souvenirs. Valladolid's is authentic Mexican.

Pirámide: Pyramid—a similar spelling but very different pronunciation: *pee-RAH-mee-deh*.

Quinta Av: Playa del Carmen's main drag, a pedestrian street that follows the beach. It's good for drinks but isn't the best place to eat Mexican food.

Riviera Maya: The Mayan Riviera—the Mexican Caribbean coast from Cancun to Tulum. South of Tulum is the Sian Ka'an Biosphere, a giant nature reserve.

Ruínas: Ruins, pronounced *roo-EE-nas*.

Terminal: Bus station. Pronounced with the accent on the last syllable, *ter-mee-NAL*.

Xcaret / Xel-Ha / Xplor / Etc.: Huge private nature parks between Cancun and Tulum. You'll see them advertised everywhere. They typically include swimming in *cenotes*, adventure-type activities (zip-lines, animal encounters) and all-you-can-eat food and drinks.

Xpu-Ha: A nice beach south of Playa del Carmen.

Yucatán: Refers to two things: the Yucatán Peninsula, the giant limestone thumb in southeast Mexico between the Gulf of Mexico and the Caribbean, or Yucatán state, which makes up the northern part of the peninsula. Valladolid is in Yucatán state. Cancun and Playa del Carmen are in the state of Quintana Roo.

Zócalo / Parque Central: The central square in most Latin American cities. The term *zócalo* is only used in Mexico. Valladolid's is gorgeous.

Zona Hotelera: The long stretch of beach and big resorts in Cancun. When people talk about Cancun, this is what they mean.

Links and Online Resources

General Information

- Air Travel in Mexico: https://nohaybronca.wordpress.com/2017/01/16/tips-for-flying-in-mexico-and-finding-cheap-domestic-flights/
- Bus Travel in Mexico: https://nohaybronca.wordpress.com/2014/02/23/how-to-travel-around-mexico-by-bus-for-cheap/
- Driving in Mexico: https://nohaybronca.wordpress.com/2017/01/10/driving-in-mexico-everything-you-need-to-know/
- What to Pack for a Trip to Mexico: https://nohaybronca.wordpress.com/2015/12/03/what-to-pack-for-a-trip-to-mexico/

- Safety in Mexico: https://nohaybronca.wordpress.com/2014/12/02/now-really-is-mexico-safe-or-not/
- Managing Your Money in Latin America: http://www.transitionsabroad.com/listings/travel/articles/how-to-safely-manage-money-latin-america.shtml
- Authentic Eating in Mexico: http://www.transitionsabroad.com/listings/travel/articles/guide-to-authentic-food-in-mexico.shtml
- Guide to Fruit in Mexico: http://www.transitionsabroad.com/listings/travel/articles/mexico-fruits-exotic-fresh.shtml
- Visiting Mexican markets: http://www.transitionsabroad.com/listings/travel/articles/mexico-guide-to-markets.shtml
- Basic Traveler's Spanish: https://nohaybronca.wordpress.com/2014/03/01/a-spanish-cheat-sheet-for-travelers-in-mexico/
- Your Chiapas Adventure: San Cristobal de las Casas and Palenque, Mexico: https://nohaybronca.wordpress.com/2017/01/05/my-guidebook-to-san-cristobal-de-las-casas-and-palenque-chiapas-mexico/

Transportation

- ADO bus: https://www.ado.com.mx/ado2/#/
- Ultramar ferry: https://www.ultramarferry.com/en
- El Caribe ferry: http://www.barcoscaribe.com
- Cancun airport terminals: http://www.cancun-airport.com/airlines-directory.htm

Finding Hotels

- Google Maps:
    https://www.google.com/maps
- Booking.com:
    http://www.booking.com/index.html?aid=1229757
- Expedia:
    https://www.expedia.com
- Tripadvisor:
    https://www.tripadvisor.com
- Airbnb:
    https://www.airbnb.com

Cancun

- El Rey Ruins:
    inah.gob.mx/es/zonas/95-zona-arqueologica-el-rey
- San Miguelito Ruins (Mayan Museum):
    inah.gob.mx/es/zonas/167-zona-arqueologica-de-san-miguelito
- La Isla Shopping Mall:
    http://www.laislacancun.mx
- The Interactive Aquarium:
    www.interactiveaquariumcancun.com/en/
- Luxury Avenue (Kukulcan Plaza):
    http://luxuryavenue.com/en/
- Cancun Scenic Tower:
    http://www.xcaret.com/scenic-tower.php
- Adventure Bay:
    www.adventurebay-cancun.com

- Delphinus Punta Cancun:
    https://www.delphinusworld.com/en/swim-with-dolphins-in-hyatt-ziva-cancun
- Aquaworld:
    https://aquaworld.com.mx/en/
- MUSA—Underwater Museum of Art:
    musamexico.org
- Cancun Golf Club at Pok ta Pok:
    http://cancungolfclub.com
- Wet 'n Wild Water Park:
    http://www.wetnwildcancun.com/about-us/
- Xochimilco Cancun:
    http://www.xoximilco.com/en/
- Croco Cun Zoo:
    http://crococunzoo.com

Valladolid

- Casa de los Venados:
    http://www.casadelosvenados.com
- Mesón de Marqués:
    https://www.mesondelmarques.com/
- Taberna de los Frailes:
    http://tabernadelosfrailes.com
- Chichén Itzá Night Show:
    http://nochesdekukulkan.com

Playa del Carmen and Mayan Riviera

- 3D Museum of Wonders:
    http://3dmuseumofwonders.com

- L'Aquarium Playa del Carmen:
    https://www.facebook.com/pg/
    LAquariumPlayaDelCarmen/
- BPM Festival:
    http://thebpmfestival.com
- Riviera Maya Jazz Festival:
    http://rivieramayajazzfestival.com
- Joya: Teatro Cirque du Soleil:
    https://www.cirquedusoleil.com/joya
- Rancho Bonanza:
    http://www.ranchobonanzacancun.com
- Xcaret:
    http://www.xcaret.com
- Xplor:
    http://www.xplor.travel/
- Xel-Ha:
    http://www.xelha.com/
- Rio Secreto:
    http://www.riosecreto.com
- Punta Venado Bike Park:
    http://www.pvbikepark.com
- Kantun-Chi Ecopark:
    http://www.kantunchi.com/
- BioParque Lu'um Balam:
    http://www.luumbalam.com
- Aktun Chen Park:
    http://aktun-chen.com
- Xcacel Beach Campground :
    http://www.cavelands.net/turtle-beach/
- Boca del Puma Adventure Park:
    http://www.bocadelpuma.com

- Akumal Ecological Center:
    http://ceakumal.org
- Akumal Dive Shop:
    http://www.akumaldiveshop.com
- Cenote Dos Ojos:
    http://www.cenotedosojos.com
- Tulum:
    http://www.inah.gob.mx/es/zonas/99-zona-arqueologica-de-tulum

About the Author

Ted Campbell

Thank you for buying this guide. Please send any questions, suggestions, or problems to NoHayBroncaBlog@gmail.com.

Also, I would appreciate it if you would review this itinerary on Amazon.

I am a freelance writer, translator, and university teacher in Mexico. I was born in Michigan and grew up in Toronto and other places in the Midwest, finally graduating from the University of Wisconsin-Milwaukee in 2002. Since then I have lived in Seoul, Vancouver, and now Mexico.

Besides traveling the world, I enjoy playing guitar and riding bicycles. Each year I usually spend two or three months traveling in southern Mexico and Central America while the university where I teach is on break.

I have written two guidebooks for Unanchor, the first for Cancun and the Mayan Riviera and the second for San Cristobal de las Casas and Palenque in the Mexican state of Chiapas.

For more travel tips and stories, please visit my blog *No Hay Bronca*. Thanks again and happy travels!

Twitter: @NoHayBroncaBlog

Blog: https://nohaybronca.wordpress.com/

Unanchor
Chief Itinerary Coordinator

Unanchor wants your opinion!

Your next travel adventure starts now. A simple review on Amazon will grant you and a travel buddy, friend, or human of your choosing any of the wonderful Unanchor digital itineraries for free.

What a deal!

Leave a Review

- Leave a review: http://www.amazon.com/unanchor

Collect your guides

- Send an email to reviews@unanchor.com with a link to your review.
- Wait with bated breath.
- Receive your new travel adventure in your inbox!

Other Unanchor Itineraries

Africa

- One Day in Africa - A Guide to Tangier
- Cape Town - What not to miss on a 4-day first-timers' itinerary
- Johannesburg/Pretoria: A 4-Day South Africa Tour Itinerary

Asia

- 4 Days in Bishkek On a Budget
- Beijing Must Sees, Must Dos, Must Eats - 3-Day Tour Itinerary
- 2 Days in Shanghai: A Budget-Conscious Peek at Modern China
- A 3-Day Tryst with 300-Year-Old Kolkata
- Kolkata (Calcutta): 2 Days of Highlights
- 3-Day Budget Delhi Itinerary
- Delhi in 3 Days - A Journey Through Time
- 3 Days Highlights of Mumbai
- Nozawa Onsen's Winter Secrets - A 3-Day Tour
- 3-Day Highlights of Tokyo
- Tour Narita During an Airport Layover
- 3 Days in the Vibrant City of Seoul and the Serene Countryside of Gapyeong
- A First Timer's Weekend Guide to Ulaanbaatar
- The Very Best of Moscow in 3 Days
- Saint Petersburg in Three Days

Central America and the Caribbean

- Old San Juan, Puerto Rico 2-Day Walking Itinerary
- Two Exciting Days in Dutch Sint Maarten - Hello Cruisers!
- Two Amazing Days in St. Croix, USVI - Hello Cruisers!

Europe

- Beginner's Iceland - A four-day self-drive itinerary
- Mostar - A City with Soul in 1 Day
- 3 Days in Brussels - The grand sites via the path less trodden
- Zagreb For Art Lovers: A Three-Day Itinerary
- 3-Day Prague Beer Pilgrimage
- Best of Prague - 3-Day Itinerary
- 3 Days in Copenhagen - Explore Like a Local
- Best of Copenhagen 2-Day Walking Itinerary
- Christmas in Copenhagen - A 2-Day Guide
- 3 Days in Helsinki
- Highlights of Budapest in 3 Days
- 3 Days in Dublin City - City Highlights, While Eating & Drinking Like a Local
- Weekend Break: Tbilisi - Crown Jewel of the Caucasus
- 2 Days In Berlin On A Budget
- A 3-Day Guide to Berlin, Germany
- 3 Days of Fresh Air in Moldova's Countryside
- Amsterdam 3-Day Alternative Tour: Not just the Red Light District
- Amsterdam Made Easy: A 3-Day Guide
- Two-day tour of Utrecht: the smaller, less touristy Amsterdam!
- Krakow: Three-Day Tour of Poland's Cultural Capital
- Best of Warsaw 2-Day Itinerary
- Lisbon in 3 Days: Budget Itinerary
- Braşov - Feel the Pulse of Transylvania in 3 Days
- Lausanne 1-Day Tour Itinerary
- Belgrade: 7 Days of History on Foot

France

- Paris to Chartres Cathedral: 1-Day Tour Itinerary
- A 3-Day Tour of Mont St Michel, Normandy and Brittany
- Art Lovers' Paris: A 2-Day Artistic Tour of the City of Lights
- Paris 1-Day Itinerary - Streets of Montmartre
- Paris 3-Day Walking Tour: See Paris Like a Local
- Paris 4-Day Winter Wonderland
- Paris for Free: 3 Days
- The Best of Paris in One Day

Greece

- Athens 3-Day Highlights Tour Itinerary
- Chania & Sfakia, Greece & Great Day Trips Nearby (5-Day Itinerary)
- Santorini, Greece in 3 Days: Living like a Local
- 2-Day Beach Tour: Travel like a Local in Sithonia Peninsula, Halkidiki, Greece
- Day Trip From Thessaloniki to Kassandra Peninsula, Halkidiki, Greece
- Thessaloniki, Greece - 3-Day Highlights Itinerary

Italy

- A Day on Lake Como, Italy
- 3-Day Florence Walking Tours
- Florence, Italy 3-Day Art & Culture Itinerary
- Milan Unknown - A 3-day tour itinerary
- 3 Days of Roman Adventure: spending time and money efficiently in Rome
- A 3-Day Tour Around Ancient Rome
- Discover Rome's Layers: A 3-Day Walking Tour
- See Siena in a Day
- Landscape, Food, & Trulli: 1 Week in Puglia, the Valle d'Itria, and Matera
- Three Romantic Walks in Venice

Spain

- 3-Day Highlights of Barcelona Itinerary
- FC Barcelona: More than a Club (A 1-Day Experience)
- Ibiza on a Budget - Three-Day Itinerary
- Three days exploring Logroño and La Rioja by public transport
- Málaga, Spain – 2-Day Tour from the Moors to Picasso
- Mijas - One Day Tour of an Andalucían White Village
- Two-Day Tour in Sunny Seville, Spain
- Best of Valencia 2-Day Guide

United Kingdom

- Bath: An Exploring Guide - 2-Day Itinerary
- History, Culture, and Craic: 3 Days in Belfast, Ireland
- 2-Day Brighton Best-of Walks & Activities
- Bristol in 2 Days: A Local's Guide
- Two-Day Self-Guided Walks - Cardiff

- The Best of Edinburgh: A 3-Day Journey from Tourist to Local
- 3-Day London Tour for Olympic Visitors
- An Insider's Guide to the Best of London in 3 Days
- Done London? A 3-day itinerary for off the beaten track North Norfolk
- London 1-Day Literary Highlights
- London for Free :: Three-Day Tour
- London's Historic City Wall Walk (1-2 days)
- London's South Bank - Off the Beaten Track 1-Day Tour
- London's Villages - A 3-day itinerary exploring Hampstead, Marylebone and Notting Hill
- Low-Cost, Luxury London - 3-Day Itinerary
- The 007 James Bond Day Tour of London
- MADchester - A Local's 3-Day Guide To Manchester
- One Day in Margate, UK on a Budget

Middle East

- Paphos 3-Day Itinerary: Live like a local!
- Adventure Around Amman: A 2-Day Itinerary
- Amman 2-Day Cultural Tour
- Doha 2-Day Stopover Cultural Tour
- Doha Surf and Turf: A two-day itinerary
- 3 Days as an Istanbulite: An Istanbul Itinerary
- Between the East and the West, a 3-Day Istanbul Itinerary

North America

Canada

- Relax in Halifax for Two Days Like a Local
- An Insider's Guide to Toronto: Explore the City Less Traveled in Three Days
- The Best of Toronto - 2-Day Itinerary
- Toronto: A Multicultural Retreat (3-day itinerary)

Mexico

- Cancun and Mayan Riviera 5-Day Itinerary (3rd Edition)
- Everything to see or do in Mexico City - 7-Day Itinerary
- Mexico City 3-Day Highlights Itinerary
- Todo lo que hay que ver o hacer en la Ciudad de México - Itinerario de 7 Días
- Your Chiapas Adventure: San Cristobal de las Casas and Palenque, Mexico 5-Day Itinerary

United States

East Coast

- Girls' 3-Day Weekend Summer Getaway in Asheville, NC
- Atlanta 3-Day Highlights
- Baltimore: A Harbor, Parks, History, Seafood & Art - 3-Day Itinerary
- Boston 2-Day Historic Highlights Itinerary
- Navigating Centuries of Boston's Nautical History in One Day
- Rainy Day Boston One-Day Itinerary
- Brooklyn, NY 2-Day Foodie Tour
- The Weekenders Guide To Burlington, Vermont
- A Local's Guide to the Hamptons 3 Day Itinerary
- Weekend Day Trip from New York City: The Wine & Whiskey Trail
- 2 Days Exploring Haunted Key West
- 3 Day PA Dutch Country Highlights (Lancaster County, PA)
- Day Trek Along the Hudson River
- A Local's Guide to Montauk, New York in 2 Days - From the Ocean to the Hills
- New Haven Highlights: Art, Culture & History 3-Day Itinerary
- Day Trip from New York City: Mountains, Falls, & a Funky Town
- 3-Day Amazing Asian Food Tour of New York City!
- Hidden Bars of New York City's East Village & Lower East Side: A 2-Evening Itinerary
- Jewish New York in Two Days
- Lower Key, Lower Cost: Lower Manhattan - 1-Day Itinerary
- New York City - First Timer's 2-Day Walking Tour
- New York City's Lower East Side, 1-Day Tour Itinerary
- New York Like A Native: Five Boroughs in Six Days
- 3-Day Discover Orlando Itinerary

- Five Days in the Wild Outer Banks of North Carolina
- Two Days in Philadelphia
- Pittsburgh: Three Days Off the Beaten Path
- Day Trip from New York City: Heights of the Hudson Valley (Bridges and Ridges)
- RVA Haunts, History, and Hospitality: Three Days in Richmond, Virginia
- Savannah 3-Day Highlights Itinerary
- Three Days in the Sunshine City of St. Petersburg, Florida
- Washington, DC in 4 Days
- Washington, DC: 3 Days Like a Local

Central US

- A Laid-Back Long Weekend in Austin, TX
- 3-Day Chicago Highlights Itinerary
- 6-Hour "Layover" Chicago
- Chicago Food, Art and Funky Neighborhoods in 3 Days
- Famous Art & Outstanding Restaurants in Chicago 1-Day Itinerary
- Family Weekend in Columbus, OH
- Ohio State Game Day Weekend
- Corpus Christi: The Insider Guide for a 4-Day Tour
- The Best of Kansas City: 3-Day Itinerary
- La Grange, Kentucky: A 3-Day Tour Itinerary
- Louisville: Three Days in Derby City
- New Orleans 3-Day Itinerary
- Paris Foodie Classics: 1 Day of French Food
- Wichita From Cowtown to Air Capital in 2 Days

West Coast

- Orange County 3-Day Budget Itinerary
- Cruisin' Asbury like a Local in 1 Day
- A Day on Bainbridge Island
- Beverly Hills, Los Angeles - 1-Day Tour
- Beer Lovers 3-Day Guide To Northern California
- The Best of Boulder, CO: A Three-Day Guide
- Lesser-known Oahu in 4 Days on a Budget
- Local's Guide to Oahu - 3-Day Tour Itinerary
- Summer in Jackson Hole: Local Tips for the Perfect Three to Five Day Adventure
- Tackling 10 Must-Dos on the Big Island in 3 Days
- Las Vegas - Gaming Destination Diversions - Ultimate 3-Day Itinerary

- Las Vegas on a Budget - 3-Day Itinerary
- 2-Day Los Angeles Vegan and Vegetarian Foodie Itinerary
- Downtown Los Angeles 1-Day Walking Tour
- Hollywood, Los Angeles - 1-Day Walking Tour
- Los Angeles 4-Day Itinerary (partly using Red Tour Bus)
- Los Angeles Highlights 3-Day Itinerary
- Los Angeles On A Budget - 4-Day Tour Itinerary
- Sunset Strip, Los Angeles - 1-Day Walking Tour
- An Active 2-3 Days In Moab, Utah
- Beyond the Vine: 2-Day Napa Tour
- Wine, Food, and Fun: 3 Days in Napa Valley
- Palm Springs, Joshua Tree & Salton Sea: A 3-Day Itinerary
- Portland Bike and Bite: A 2-Day Itinerary
- Three Days Livin' as a True and Local Portlander
- Weekend Tour of Portland's Craft Breweries, Wineries, & Distilleries
- Best of the Best: Three-Day San Diego Itinerary
- San Francisco 2-Day Highlights Itinerary
- San Francisco Foodie Weekend Itinerary
- The Tech Lover's 48-Hour Travel Guide to Silicon Valley & San Francisco
- Alaska Starts Here - 3 Days in Seward
- Three Days in Central California's Wine Country
- Tucson: 3 Days at the Intersection of Mexico, Native America & the Old West

Oceania

- The Blue Mountains: A weekend of nature, culture and history.
- A Weekend Snapshot of Melbourne
- An Afternoon & Evening in Melbourne's Best Hidden Bars
- Laneway Melbourne: A One-Day Walking Tour
- Magic of Melbourne 3-Day Tour
- Two Wheels and Pair of Cozzies: the Best of Newcastle in 3 Days
- Best of Perth's Most Beautiful Sights in 3 Days
- A Weekend Snapshot of Sydney
- Sydney, Australia - 3-Day **Best Of** Itinerary
- Enjoy the Rebuild - Christchurch 2-Day Tour
- The Best of Wellington: 3-Day Itinerary

South America

- An Insider's Guide to the Best of Buenos Aires in 3 Days
- Buenos Aires Best Kept Secrets: 2-Day Itinerary
- Sights & Sounds of São Paulo - 3-Day Itinerary
- Cuenca, Ecuador - A 3-Day Discovery Tour
- A 1-Day Foodie's Dream Tour of Arequipa
- Arequipa - A 2-Day Itinerary for First-Time Visitors
- Cusco and the Sacred Valley - a five-day itinerary for a first-time visitor
- Little Known Lima 3-Day Tour

Southeast Asia

- Between the Skyscrapers - Hong Kong 3-Day Discovery Tour
- Art and Culture in Ubud, Bali – 1-Day Highlights
- Go with the Sun to Borobudur & Prambanan in 1 Day
- A 3-Day Thrilla in Manila then Flee to the Sea
- Manila on a Budget: 2-Day Itinerary
- A First Timer's Guide to 3 Days in the City that Barely Sleeps - Singapore
- Family Friendly Singapore - 3 Days in the Lion City
- Singapore: 3 Fun-Filled Days on this Tiny Island
- The Affordable Side of Singapore: A 4-Day Itinerary
- The Two Worlds of Kaohsiung in 5 Days
- 72 Hours in Taipei: The All-rounder
- Girls' Weekend in Bangkok: Shop, Spa, Savour, Swoon
- The Ins and Outs of Bangkok: A 3-Day Guide
- Saigon 3-Day Beyond the Guidebook Itinerary

Unanchor is a global family for travellers to experience the world with the heart of a local.

Printed in Poland
by Amazon Fulfillment
Poland Sp. z o.o., Wrocław